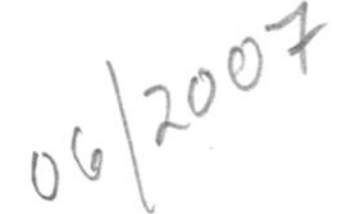

101 your child will spell by the end of Grade 1

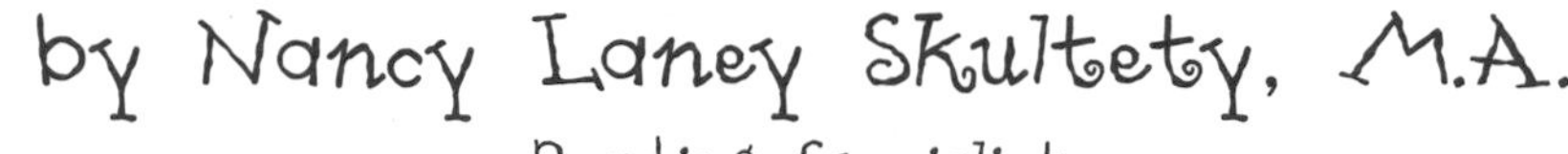
by Nancy Laney Skultety, M.A.
Reading Specialist
Homer-Center School District
Homer City, Pennsylvania

BARRON'S

With love and thanks to my friends, Karen Sanguigni, Lois Bartko, Betty Ann Pavlick, Bonnie Skibo, Terri Koenigsberg, Michael Gentile, and Beverly Mastalski, for their help and support. Also with love and special thanks to my family Terry, Breanne, Kolby, and Keely for their patience.

Special thanks are given to Michael Mastalski for his thoughts and wonderful sketches, and to everyone at Barron's Educational Series for believing in my work.

All inquiries should be addressed to:
Barron's Educational Series, Inc.
250 Wireless Boulevard
Hauppauge, New York 11788
http: //www.barronseduc.com

ISBN-13: 978-0-7641-3538-5 (book)
ISBN-10: 0-7641-3538-4 (book)

ISBN-13: 978-0-7641-8347-8 (CD-ROM)
ISBN-10: 0-7641-8347-8 (CD-ROM)

ISBN-13: 978-0-7641-7948-8 (package)
ISBN-10: 0-7641-7948-9 (package)

Printed in China

9 8 7 6 5 4 3 2 1

Dear Special Folks at Home:

You have chosen this book because you are committed to enhancing your child's ability to spell words correctly. Your concern will have a positive impact on your child's ability to use correct spelling and on his or her ability to communicate in writing, thereby improving his or her academic success.

Thank you for selecting this book to use as a teaching/learning tool. My hope is that the special child in your life will enjoy and also learn from the spelling activities found in this book. Additionally, I hope you, the adult, will experience joy as you see your child attain spelling mastery of the 101 target words.

This book contains fun learning activities that will provide your child with the practice needed to have mastery of 101 non-decodable spelling words. The words chosen for practice were done so because they do not follow typical spelling patterns. These 101 words are generally difficult for children to spell, but with practice your child will have command of them and will be able to write more effectively.

Additionally, a CD-ROM is included to allow your child to practice each spelling word using fun, interactive games and activities.

Successful spellers are confident writers. I hope the activities found in this book motivate your child to write with confidence. The more a child is exposed to these words the better speller he or she will become.

Sincerely,

Nancy Laney Skultety

Nancy Laney Skultety

Contents

Cumulative Word List

about
again
all
always
animal
answer
any
are
around
as
away
ball
because
book
both
brother
buy
by
circle
climb
color
come
could
do
does
down
draw
every
eye
family
father
find
food
friend
full
give
good
great
guess
have
house
how
kind
know
laugh
lion
look
lose
love
many
money
mother
move
my
new
now
of
oh
old
once
one
only
our
out
picture
poor
pretty
put
said
saw
says
school
shoes
some
soon
story
talk
the
their
there
they
to
too
took
through
very
walk
want
was
watch
water
were
what
where
who
won
would
write
you
your
zoo

Spelling Tips

1. Look at the word

2. Say it

3. Study its letters and its shape

4. Write the word

5. Cover the word

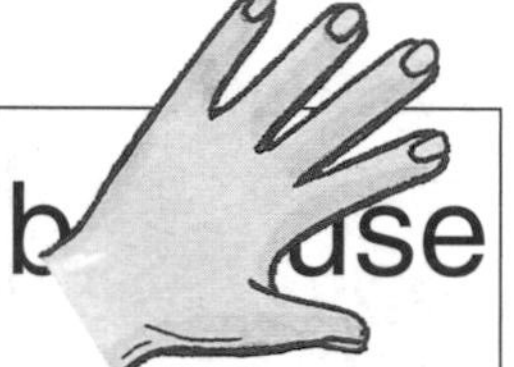

6. Visualize the word

7. Say each letter in the word

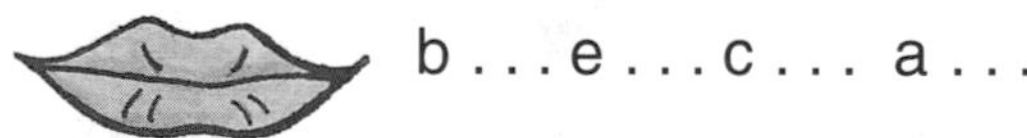

8. Write the word

9. Uncover the word to check it

10. If incorrect repeat

Learners rely on their senses to help them acquire knowledge; therefore, it is sound practice to engage as many senses as possible in the learning process.

The common learning modes are:

1. Visual

2. Auditory

3. Tactile—Kinesthetic

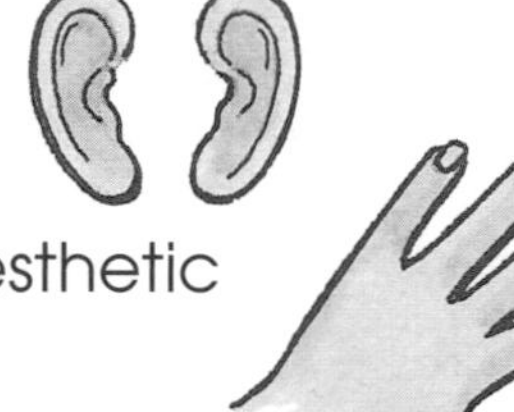

The Visual learning mode utilizes the eyes and supports learning through seeing.

The Auditory mode utilizes sound and supports learning through sound.

The Tactile—Kinesthetic mode utilizes touch/movement and supports learning through manipulation/movement.

Learning to spell words using a variety of learning modes is fun!

Suggested activities to foster Visual Learning include the following:

— Word Detective—find and highlight spelling words in print
— Look at word shape
— Illustrate the word
— Change letter font, size, and color as the word is practiced
— Break the word into sections (an example, coverage—cove rage)
— Study the word; look for special sounds, double letters, and prefixes/suffixes

— Cover the word and attempt to spell using visual memory

Suggested activities to foster Auditory Learning include the following:

— Hear the word, and then spell it aloud letter by letter
— Chant out the letters to spell the word
— Use a tape recorder to spell out each word then listen repeatedly
— Sing the spelling word, put it to a tune
— Create sentences through using the letters in the spelling word
    (examples—
    arithmetic = A rat in Tom's house might eat Tom's ice cream.
    because = Boys eat cones always under shady elms.)

Suggested activities to foster Tactile—Kinesthetic Learning include the following:

— Move letter cards or letter tiles to spell the word
— Use magnetic or foam letters to build the word
— Write the word in finger paint, foam soap, sand, or shaving cream
— Use a paint brush and water on black construction paper or chalkboard (watch the word disappear like magic and reappear when it dries)
— Stamp the word out, use ink pad and rubber alphabet letter stamps
— Use alphabet stickers to build the word
— Write the word repeatedly
— Write the words in the air with finger
— Run finger over sandpaper letters to spell out each word
— Trace letters in the word with any writing implement
— Trace the letters on someone's back
— Cut paper letters and glue to form the spelling word
— Glue cereal or other small items to build the word
— Trace the spelling word in high pile carpet remnants
— Build the word using letter Jell-O, candy such as gummy letters, or alphabet cereal, then eat the word
— Pace or walk as the word is recited letter by letter

There are many creative ways to engage your child in learning. The use of memory aids is highly effective in helping children learn to spell. Challenge yourself and your child to create and use other memory aids.

Once your child has practiced using creative means, **please remember to test your child using the standard paper and pencil method**, because that is how it will be tested in the classroom.

Keep in mind that any time can be a spelling practice time. Practice while riding in the car (chant or sing the words), waiting at the bus stop (write the words in the air), or taking a bath (use foam soap or foam letters).

Individual Spelling Lists

Word List 1

father
out
your
friend
picture
zoo
full
poor
give
pretty

Word List 2

draw
once
would
every
only
write
around
our
you
family

Word List 3

again
guess
story
all
have
talk
always
house
the
animal

Word List 4

answer
how
their
any
kind
there
are
know
they
eye
about

Word List 5

find
good
great
put
said
saw
says
school
shoes
soon

Word List 6

brother
mother
want
buy
move
was
by
my
watch
circle

Word List 7

as
laugh
to
away
lion
too
food
look
took
ball

Word List 8

do
oh
where
does
of
who
down
old
won
one

Word List 9

lose
through
because
love
very
book
many
walk
both
money

Word List 10

climb
new
water
color
now
were
come
some
what
could

It's Picking Time

Help Farmer Joe pick apples.

Look at the apples on Farmer Joe's tree. Find the words from Word List 1 that are spelled correctly and write them on the baskets below.

Word List	
father	out
your	give
zoo	full
poor	friend
picture	pretty

Football Puzzlers

Circle the football puzzle pieces to make a football that spells each word correctly.

Word List	
father	out
your	give
zoo	full
poor	friend
picture	pretty

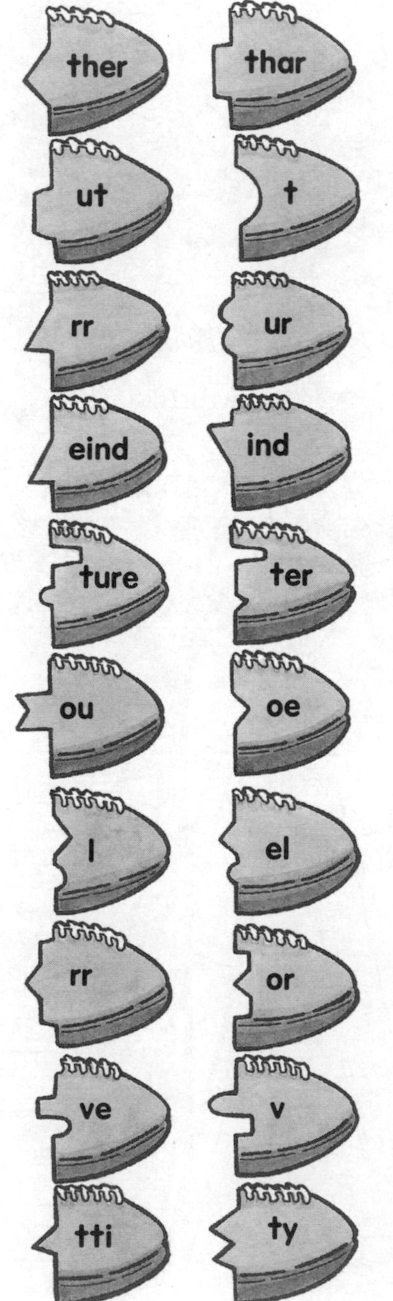

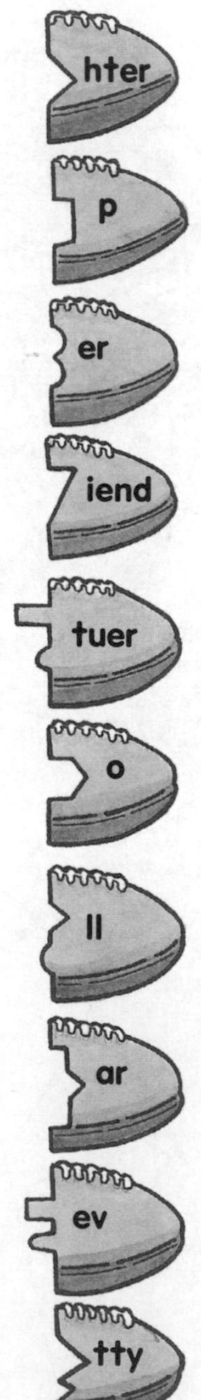

School Daze

Help Sam and Kate get through the maze to get to school. Follow the path that has all the words spelled correctly.

Word List	
father	out
your	give
zoo	full
poor	friend
picture	pretty

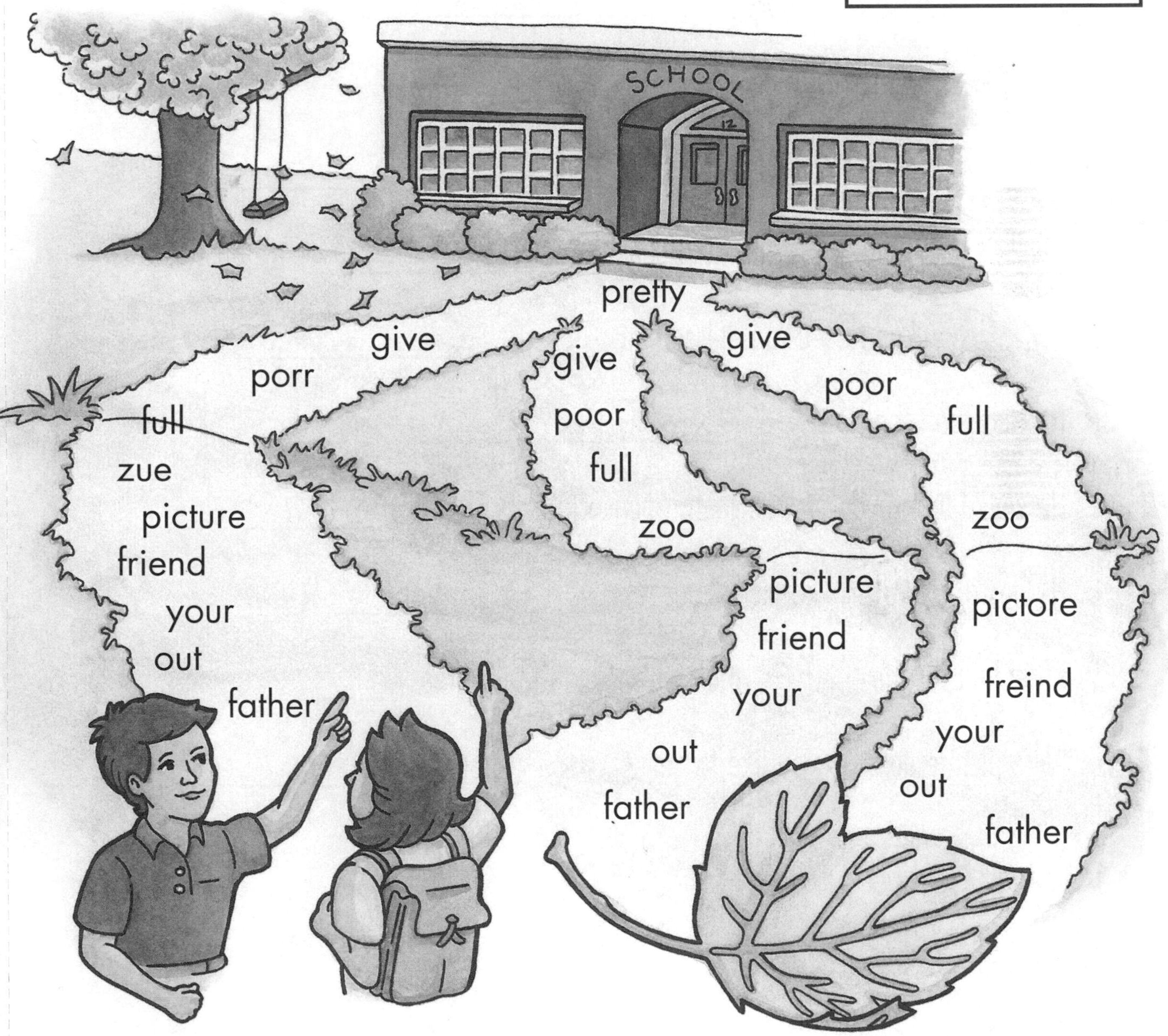

Supply the Correct Spelling Word

Use the code on the school supplies to fill in the blank with the correct spelling word.

1. I will smile for my class [scissors] . ____________________
2. My [desk] will smile, too. ____________________
3. I hope my picture turns [bus] nice. ____________________
4. I will [paper] my picture to my friend. ____________________
5. My [eraser] likes to see me dressed up. ____________________
6. He tells me I look [globe] . ____________________
7. He says I look even prettier than a peacock in the [school] . ____________
8. He has a book [glue] of pictures of me. ____________________
9. I feel bad for the [ruler] man who takes the pictures. ____________ He must get tired.
10. I like picture day. Do you like to get [books] picture taken? ____________________

Word Code

Lend a Hand

Miss Jones needs your help!
Miss Jones had to stop in the middle of making an answer key for the crossword puzzle she had the boys and girls in her class do for homework. Help her finish the answer key. Fill in the spelling word that fits in the blanks. Use the Word List to help you.

Word List	
father	out
your	give
zoo	full
poor	friend
picture	pretty

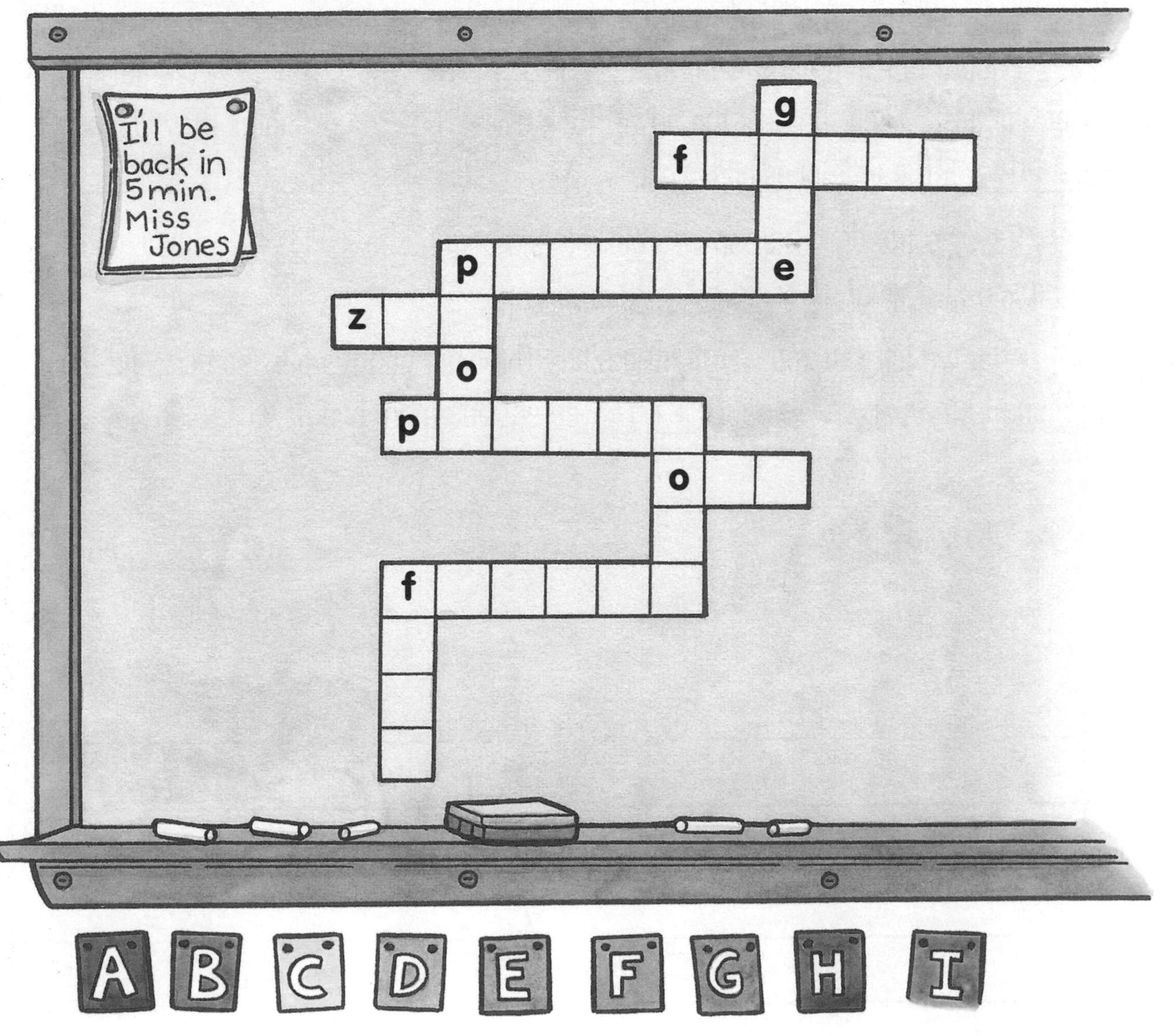

A Friendly Letter

Miss Jones is having her class write friendly letters about what they did over the summer. Help Todd finish writing his letter to Joe. Use the Word List to help you. Write the answers in the spaces below.

Word List	
father	out
your	give
zoo	full
poor	friend
picture	pretty

Dear Joe,

I had a fun summer. I went to the ____[1]____ with my____[2]____. We got to see a lot of animals. I liked the deer the best. I took a ____[3]____ of them. They looked so____[4]____. The little ones had spots.

It was a hot day. The sun was out big and bright. The ____[5]____, hairy, ape looked so hot. I wanted to ____[6]____ him a fan.

After we left the zoo we ate at a diner. The diner had the best burgers and fries. Dad, and I ate until we were too ____[7]____ to eat one more bite. It was a fun day!

____[8]____ ____[9]____,

Todd

1. ______________________
2. ______________________
3. ______________________
4. ______________________
5. ______________________
6. ______________________
7. ______________________
8. ______________________
9. ______________________

Let's Go!

Print the word over and over around the footballs or megaphones.

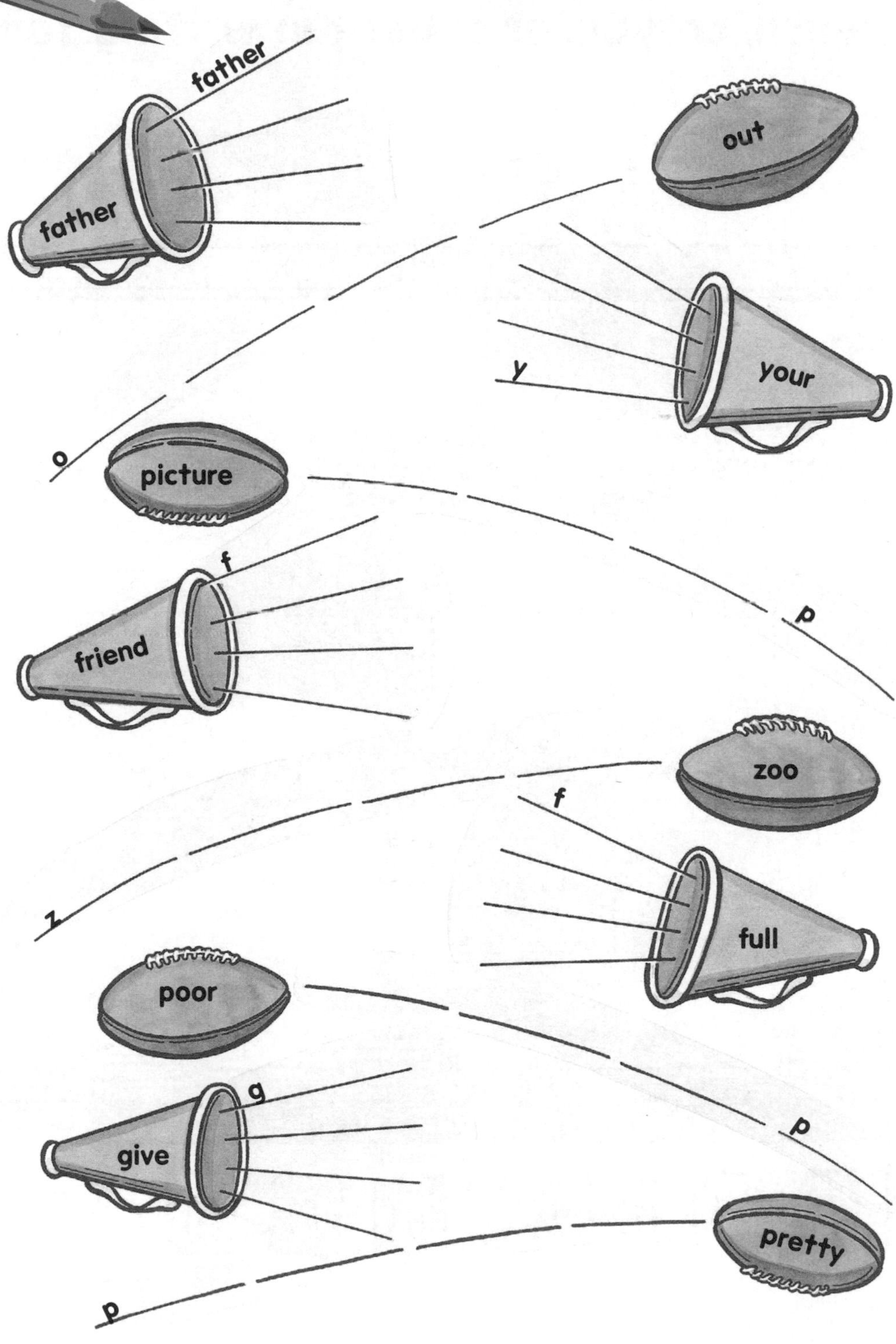

Chalk It Up!

Trace the words on the chalkboard. Use a pencil, crayon, or other fun writing tool.

Be a Word Detective!

Circle each misspelled word in the fall story. You will find 10 spelling words that are misspelled. Write each word correctly in letter shaped boxes. Use the Word List to help you.

Word List	
father	out
your	give
zoo	full
poor	friend
picture	pretty

Fall Help

"My father likes fall," said Tim. "He says the leaves are pritty."

"My fother does not like fall," said Ann. "He does not like to rake. It makes him tired, and then we have no time for fun."

"I giv him a hand, but por father is still beat," said Ann.

"Your yard is foll of trees. That makes it hard to keep it raked," said Tim. "You are my frend, Ann. I like to rake. Next time I will help your father rake."

"Good!" said Ann. "Then we will have more time to go to the zoe. Father and I love to go to the zoo. You can come with us."

"That is a deal," said Tim. "I will help the next time I see him otu raking."

"Father loves to take pictures at the zoo. He takes a pictuer of all the neat animals. I bet he will take yor picture, too."

"That is fine with me," said Tim. "I can't wait to go. I think I'll grab the rake and get going. He may want to go today!"

"I will give you a hand," said Ann with a smile. "I'm glad you are my friend. I bet my father will be glad I have a friend like you, too!"

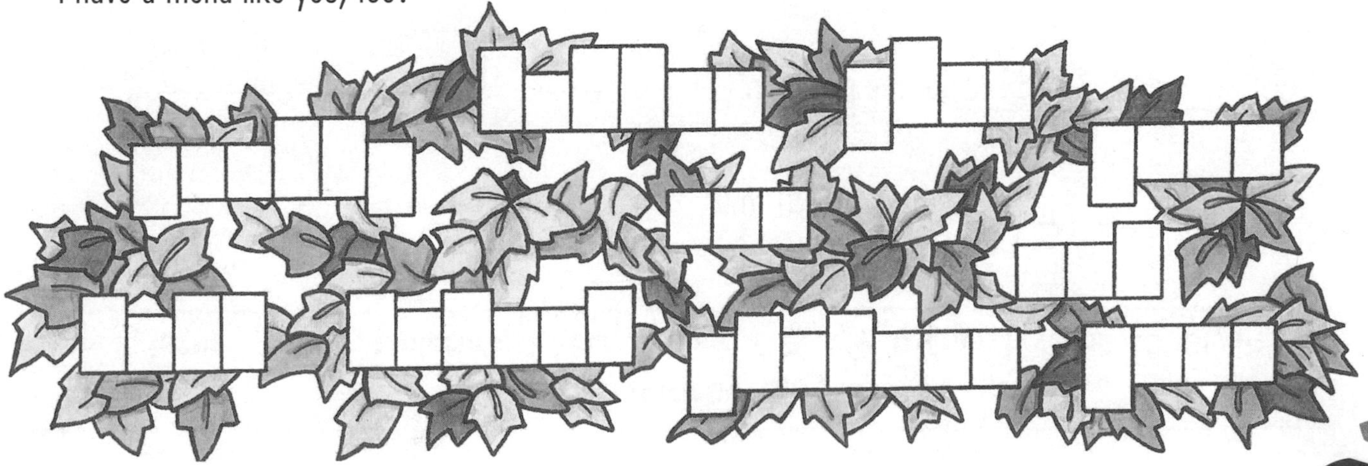

Test Time!

Think of the words in Word List 1. Read the riddles. Fill in the blank with the correct spelling word. Look at the answers below to check your spelling. Write any misspelled words 3 times each on the lines provided.

1. A ________ is a place to see animals. ________ ________ ________
2. A ________ is a dad. ________ ________ ________
3. ________ means not in. ________ ________ ________
4. A ________ is a photo. ________ ________ ________
5. ________ means belonging to you. ________ ________ ________
6. ________ means not rich. ________ ________ ________
7. ________ means not ugly. ________ ________ ________
8. ________ means a pal. ________ ________ ________
9. ________ means not empty. ________ ________ ________
10. ________ means to hand to. ________ ________ ________

Answers

1. zoo 2. father 3. Out 4. picture 5. Your 6. Poor 7. Pretty 8. Friend 9. Full 10. Give

Fall Yard Work

Luke and Jade have been busy raking leaves.

Circle the pile of leaves that has all the spelling words written correctly.

Word List	
draw	write
once	around
would	our
every	you
only	family

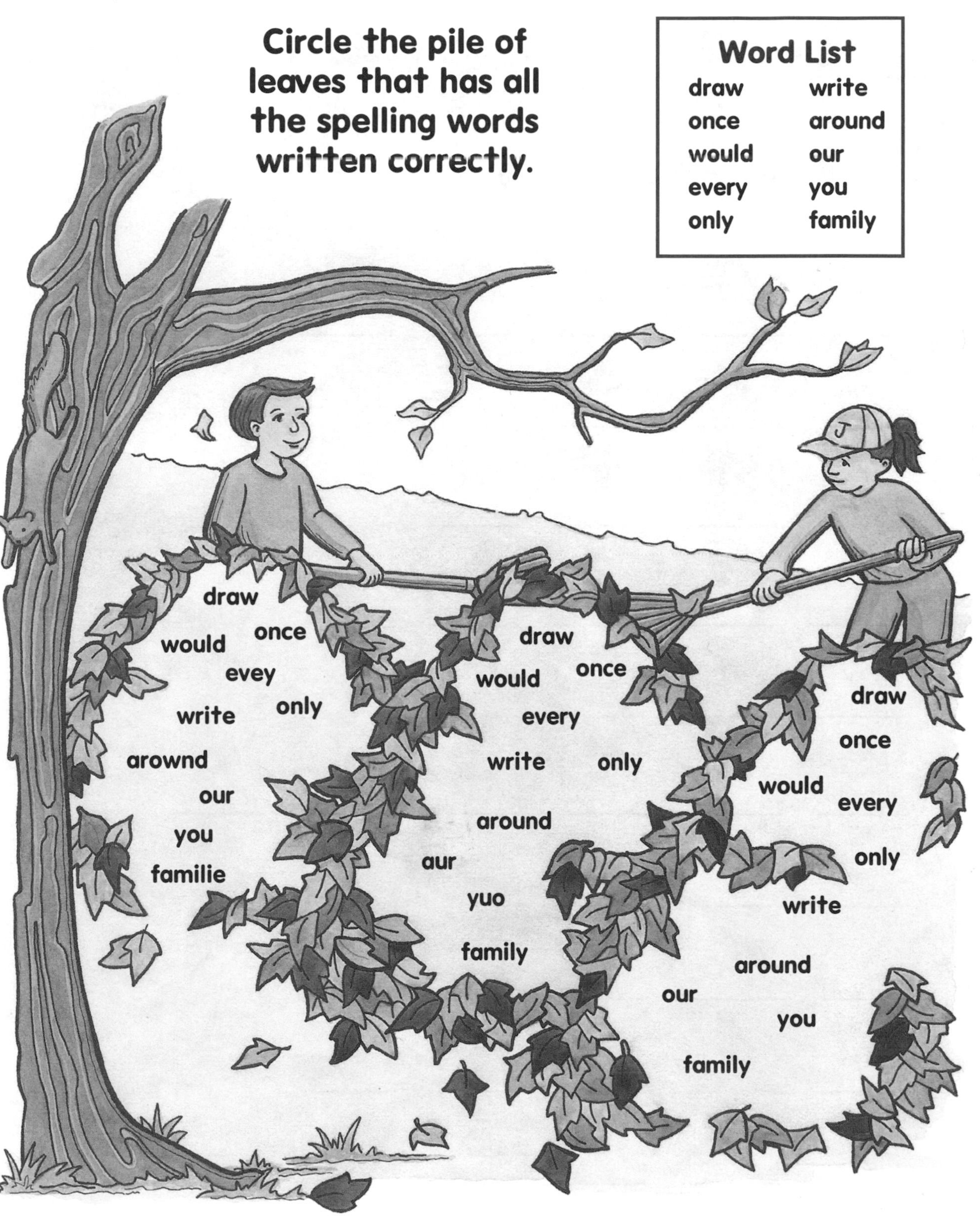

Fall Code Crackers

Use the code to write the spelling words.

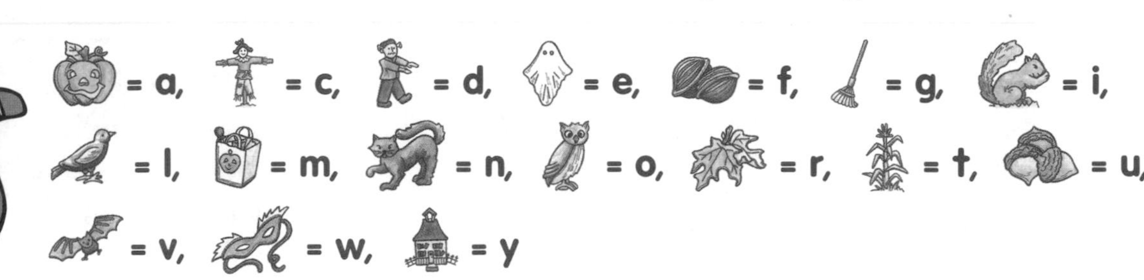

1.      
   ____ ____ ____ ____ ____ ____

2.   
   ____ ____ ____

3.    
   ____ ____ ____ ____

4.    
   ____ ____ ____ ____

5.    
   ____ ____ ____ ____

6.      
   ____ ____ ____ ____ ____ ____

7.   
   ____ ____ ____

8.     
   ____ ____ ____ ____ ____

9.     
   ____ ____ ____ ____ ____

10.     
    ____ ____ ____ ____ ____

As The Crow Flies

Unscramble the words on the crows to spell Word List 2 words. Write the word.

Word List	
draw	write
once	around
would	our
every	you
only	family

Nuts About Spelling

Help the squirrel gather tasty nuts for the winter. Find then circle the spelling words hidden on the acorns.

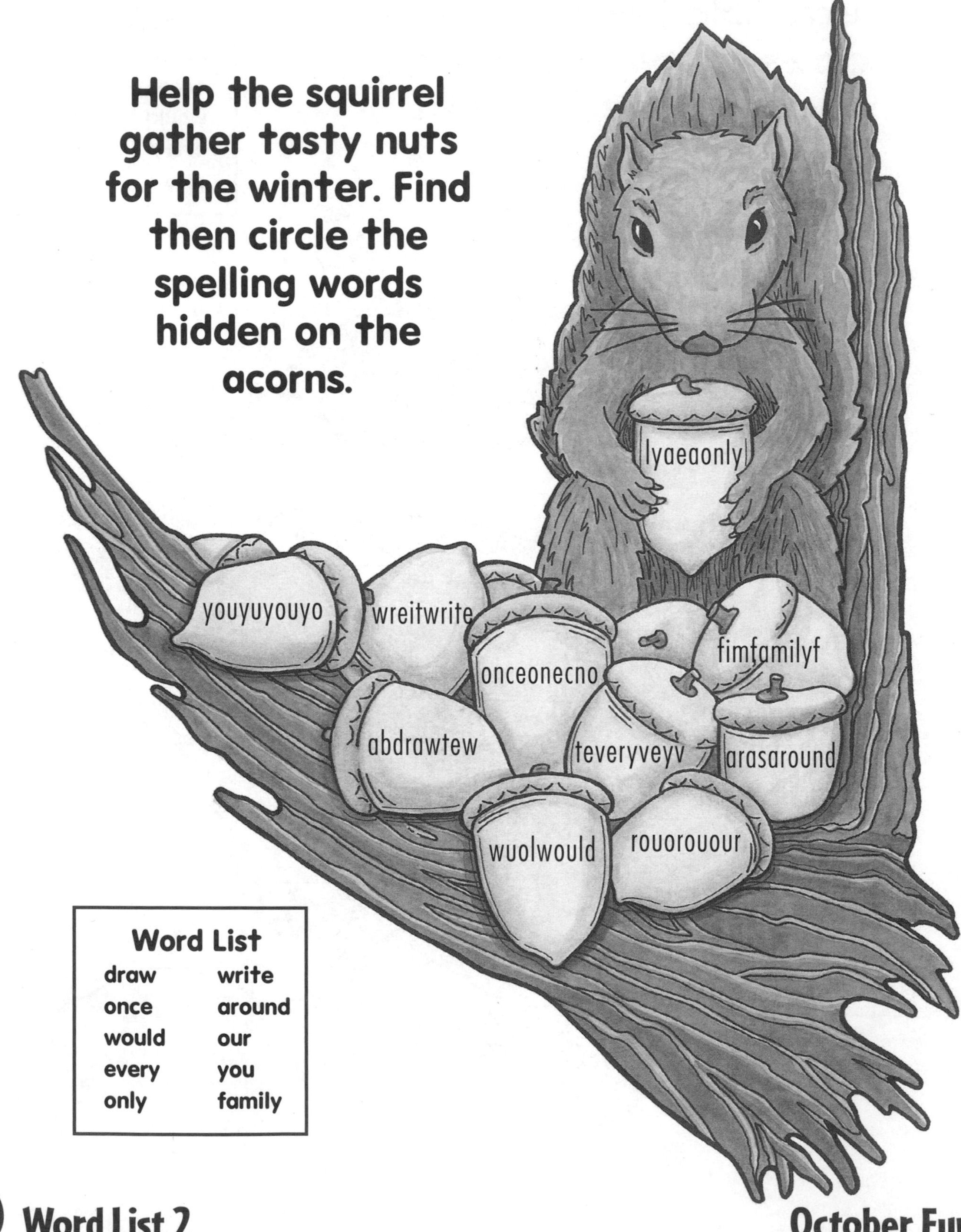

Word List

draw	write
once	around
would	our
every	you
only	family

Going Batty with Spelling

Fill in the missing letters on the bats to write the spelling words correctly. Use the Word List to help you.

Word List	
draw	write
once	around
would	our
every	you
only	family

An A-mazing Maze!

Help Sam and Dan get through the corn maze. Follow the path that has each spelling word spelled correctly.

Jack-o'-lantern Spelling

Use the code to write the spelling words around the jack-o-lantern.

Code

right triangle eye = only
left triangle eye = would
triangle nose = around
semicircle mouth = family
top tooth = you
bottom tooth = write
stem = our
leaves = every
blanket = draw
candle = once

On the Prowl!

Look at each word written beside each cat. Build each spelling word. Cut each letter to form the spelling word. Glue the letters on the black cat to spell the spelling word. Use old newspapers, magazines, and catalogs. Ask an adult for help.

draw
would
our
only
once

Five Little Jack-o'-lanterns

Look at the 5 jack-o'-lanterns sitting on the fence. Circle the one that has the spelling words spelled correctly.

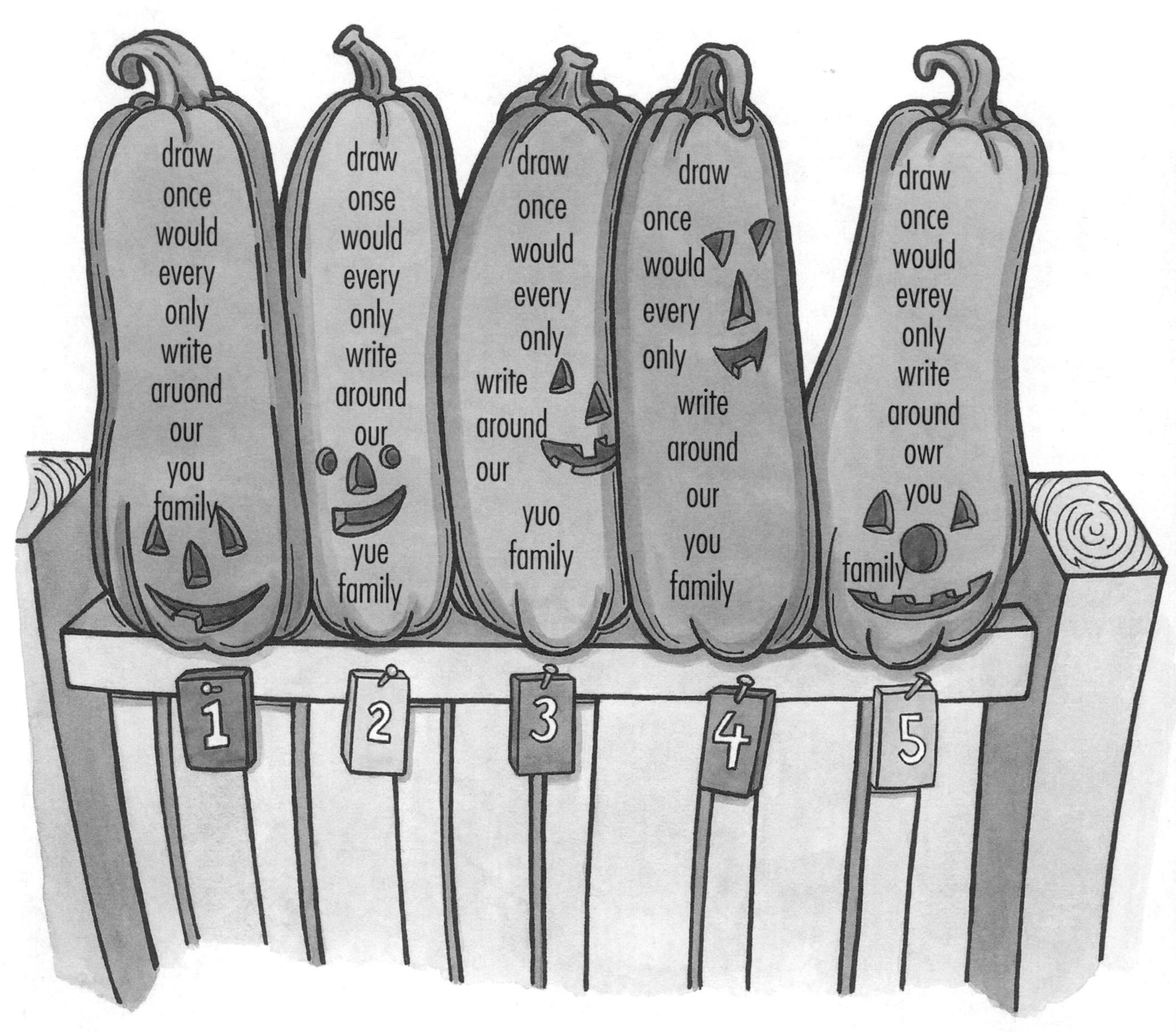

Don't Get Spooked Over Spelling!

Think of the words on Word List 2. Write the words that begin with the letters o, w, d, and f where they belong.

1. owl

____

____

____

2. werewolf

____

____

3. Dracula

____

4. Frankenstein's monster

____

Fill in the blanks with 2 spelling words you have not used.

Did _______ spell _________word right?

Answers on the following page.

Practice Time!

I hope you spelled every word correctly!

Write any misspelled words 3 times each on the lines provided.

______	______	______
______	______	______
______	______	______
______	______	______
______	______	______
______	______	______
______	______	______
______	______	______
______	______	______
______	______	______

Answers

1. once, only, our 2. would, write 3. draw 4. family

Did you spell every word right?

Shipping Out

Each November we remember that in the year 1620 the Pilgrims came to the New World in hope of a better life. They came by ship. Trace the words on each ship to form a spelling word. Then write the word beneath the ship. Use a pencil or other writing tool, such as pen, marker, crayon, or colored pencil to write each word.

Plenty to Find

What is hidden in the picture?
Use the color code to find out.

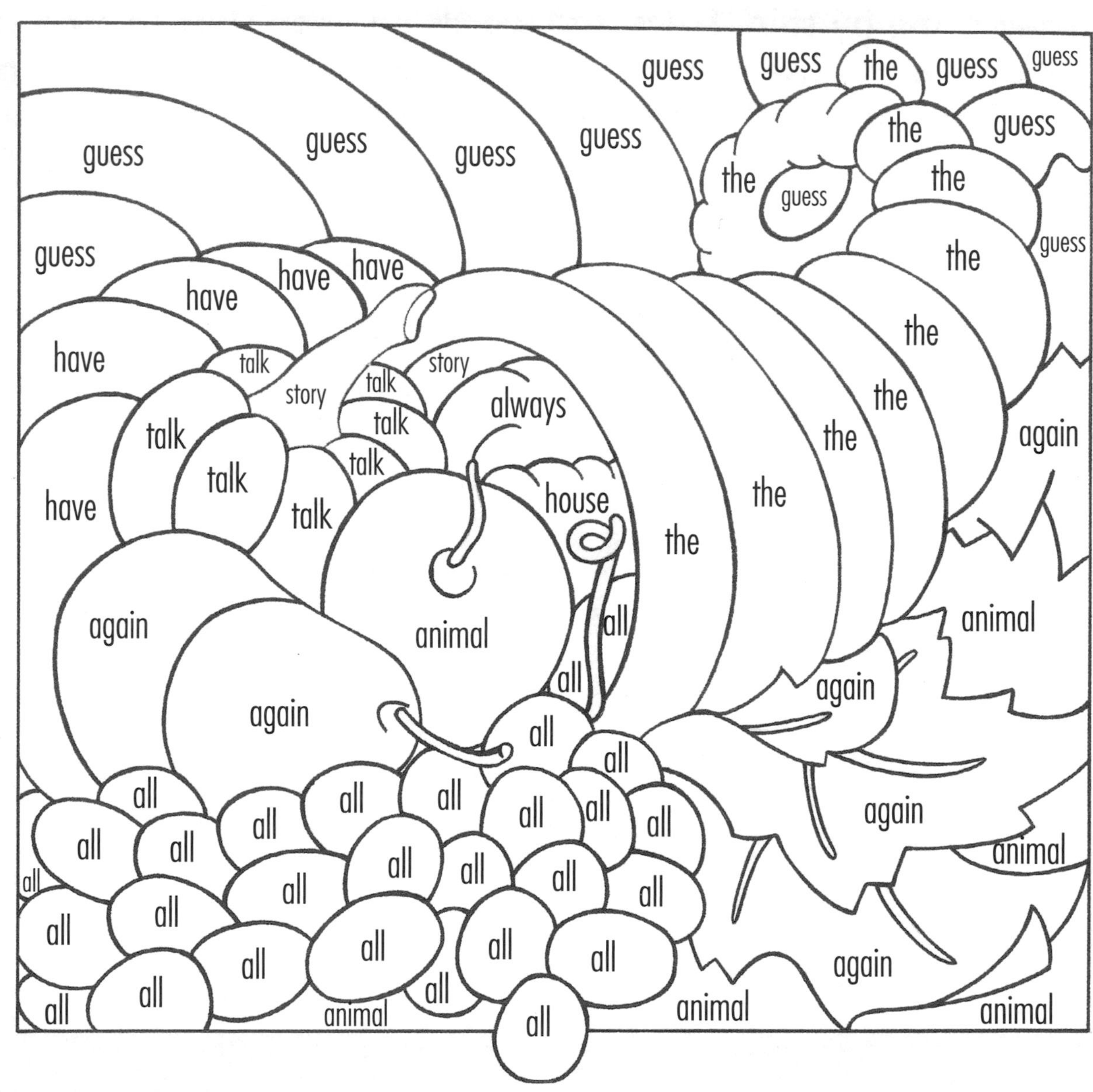

Color Code

again = light brown	**all = purple**	**always = light purple**	**the = yellow**
guess = light blue	**have = green**	**house = light orange**	**animal = red**
story = brown	**talk = orange**		

Oh, Turkey Feathers!

Look at each turkey's tail feathers. Find the spelling word written on the turkey's feathers that does not match the rest. Circle the word that does not match the rest.

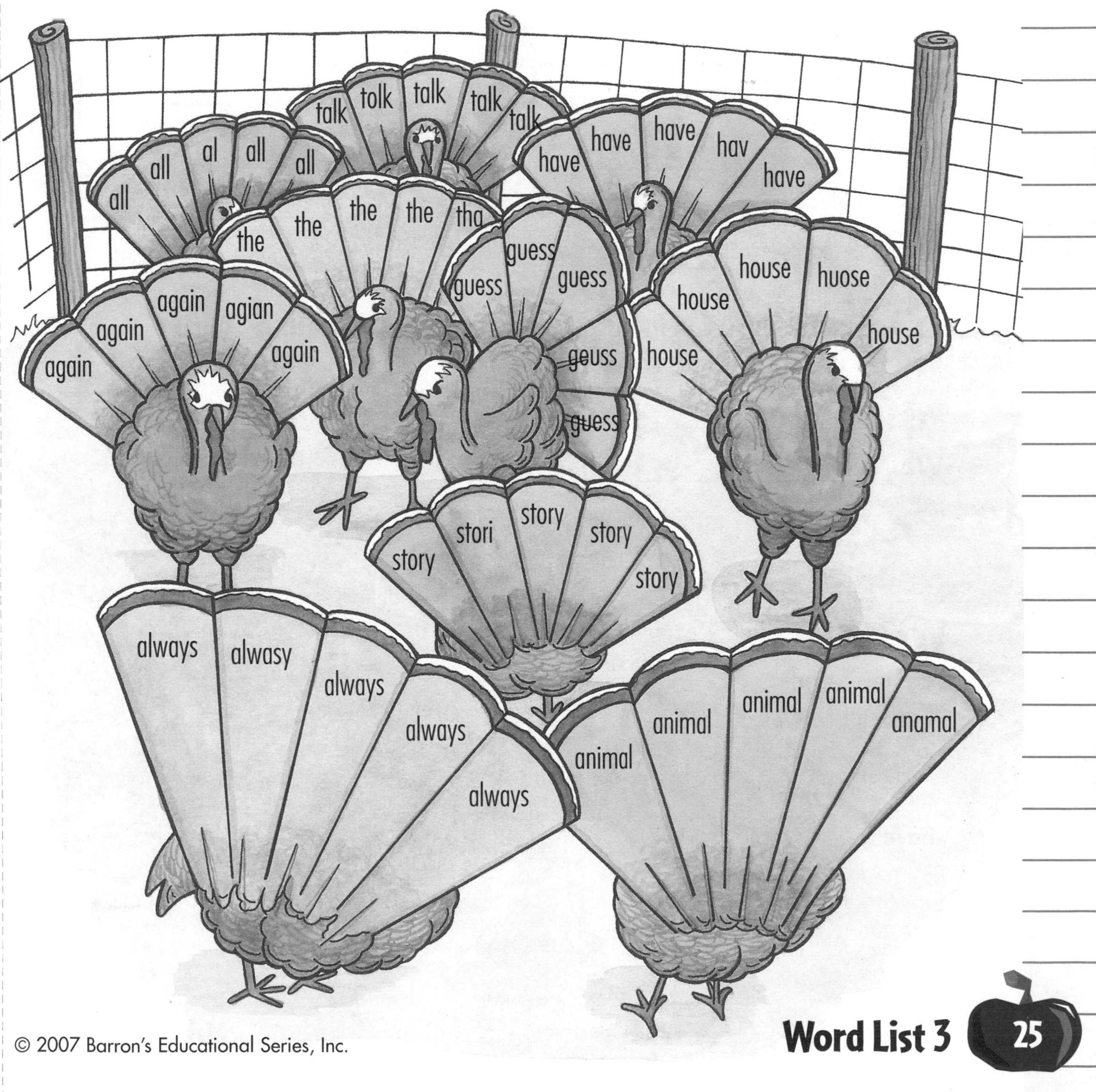

Word Feast

Read the clues to fill in the boxes. Use the Word List to help you.

1. a tale
2. a dog or a cat
3. a home
4. to chat
5. every time
6. every one

Look at the answers in the boxes. Which two spelling word answers can be used to fill in the blank?

We _________________ gather together.

We _________________ gather together.

Word List

again	talk
guess	always
story	house
all	the
have	animal

Bead Codes

Native Americans used beads made from shells as money and for ornament. The beads were called wampum.

Use the code to write the word on the beads on the necklace and on the extra beads on the table.

Code

animal =

always =

story =

have =

talk =

Code

house =

guess =

the =

all =

again =

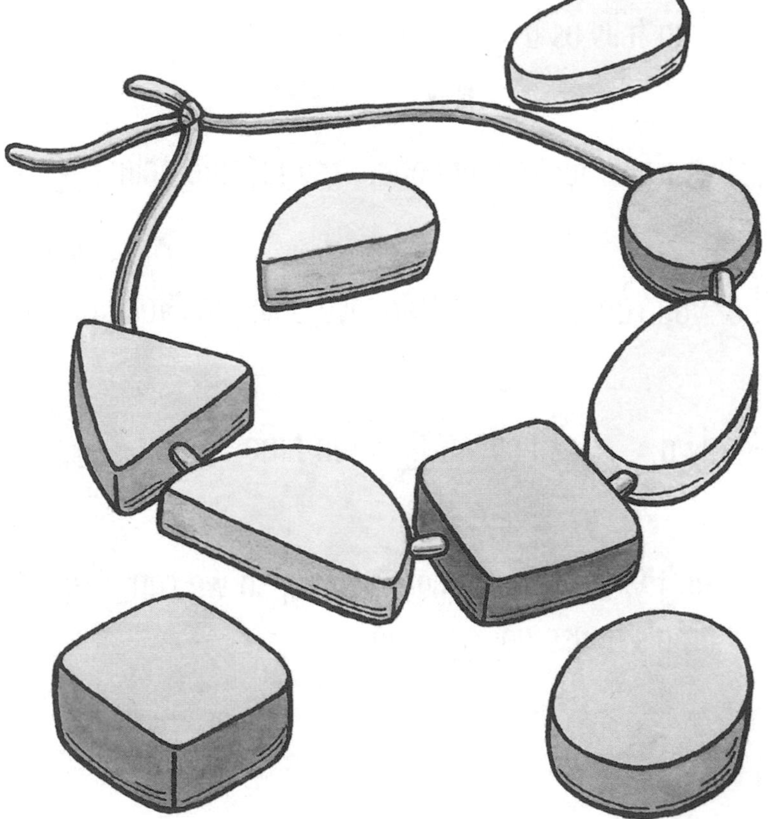

Thankful Spelling

Choose the correct letter to spell the word. Circle the letter. Then write the letter in the blank to finish the spelling word.

1. On Thanksgiving we alw_____ys have fun.

   a, i

2. _____ll the family goes to Grandma's ho_____se.

   O, A **u, o**

3. We all sit around the table and ta_____k.

   o, l

4. Grandma tells us a s_____ory after we eat.

   h, t

5. Last year she told a story about my favorite anim_____l, a fox!

   i, a

6. I bet you can g_____ess we love going to Grandma's for Thanksgiving.

   o, u

7. We alwa_____s hav_____ a fun time.

   a, y **v, e**

8. We can't wait for next Thanksgiving, so we can all get together at Grandma's house ag_____ in.

   a, e

Word List

again	talk
guess	always
story	house
all	the
have	animal

A Bountiful Harvest!

Look at the foods that have been harvested. Unscramble the words on the foods to make spelling words. Write the word in the space provided.

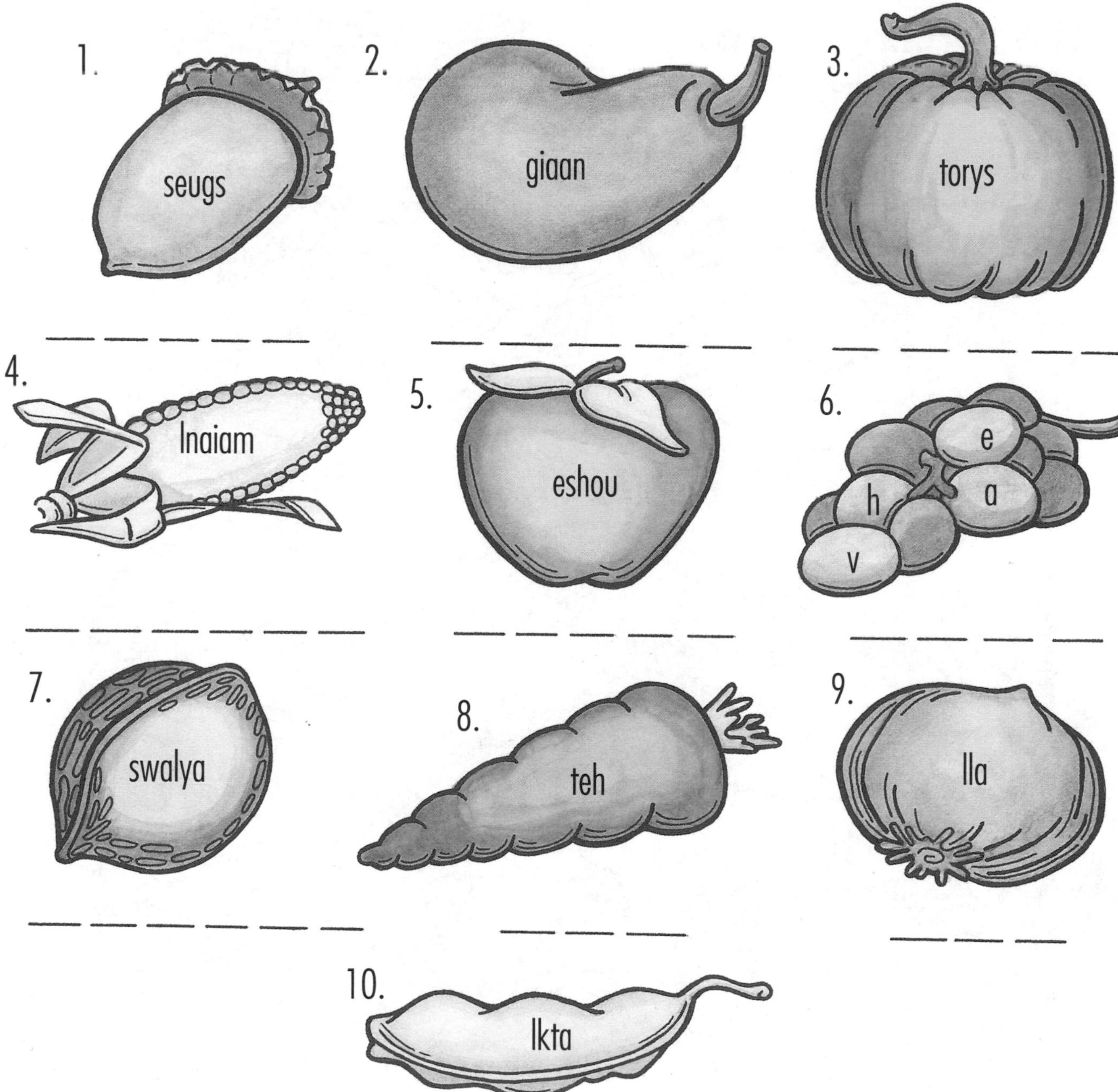

What a Catch!

Help John and Bob catch fish for the Thanksgiving feast. Circle the fish that have the spelling words spelled correctly.

always

the

hoose

guess

the

storee

alweys

gess

house

story

How many fish did they catch? Count the fish with the word written correctly. Write the number.

________ **fish**

Hats Off to the Pilgrims!

Look at the words written on each Pilgrim hat. Trace the word. Fill in the missing letters to spell the word and then write the word on each hat.

Harvest Time!

Time to show what you know!

Think about the spelling words in this practice set. Can you spell them?

Look at each horn of plenty. Write the spelling word that ends with the letter written on the horn of plenty.

Answers on the following page.

Test Time!

I hope you spelled every word correctly!

Write any misspelled words 3 times each on the lines provided.

____________	____________	____________
____________	____________	____________
____________	____________	____________
____________	____________	____________
____________	____________	____________
____________	____________	____________
____________	____________	____________
____________	____________	____________
____________	____________	____________
____________	____________	____________

Answers

l. animal, all   k. talk   e. have, the, house   y. story   s. always   n. again

Happy Holidays!

Use the December holiday words to build spelling words.

Happy Holidays! Kwanzaa, Christmas, Hanukkah

Fill in the blanks to form spelling words. Use the Word List to help you.

Word List

answer	how
their	any
kind	there
are	know
they	eye
about	

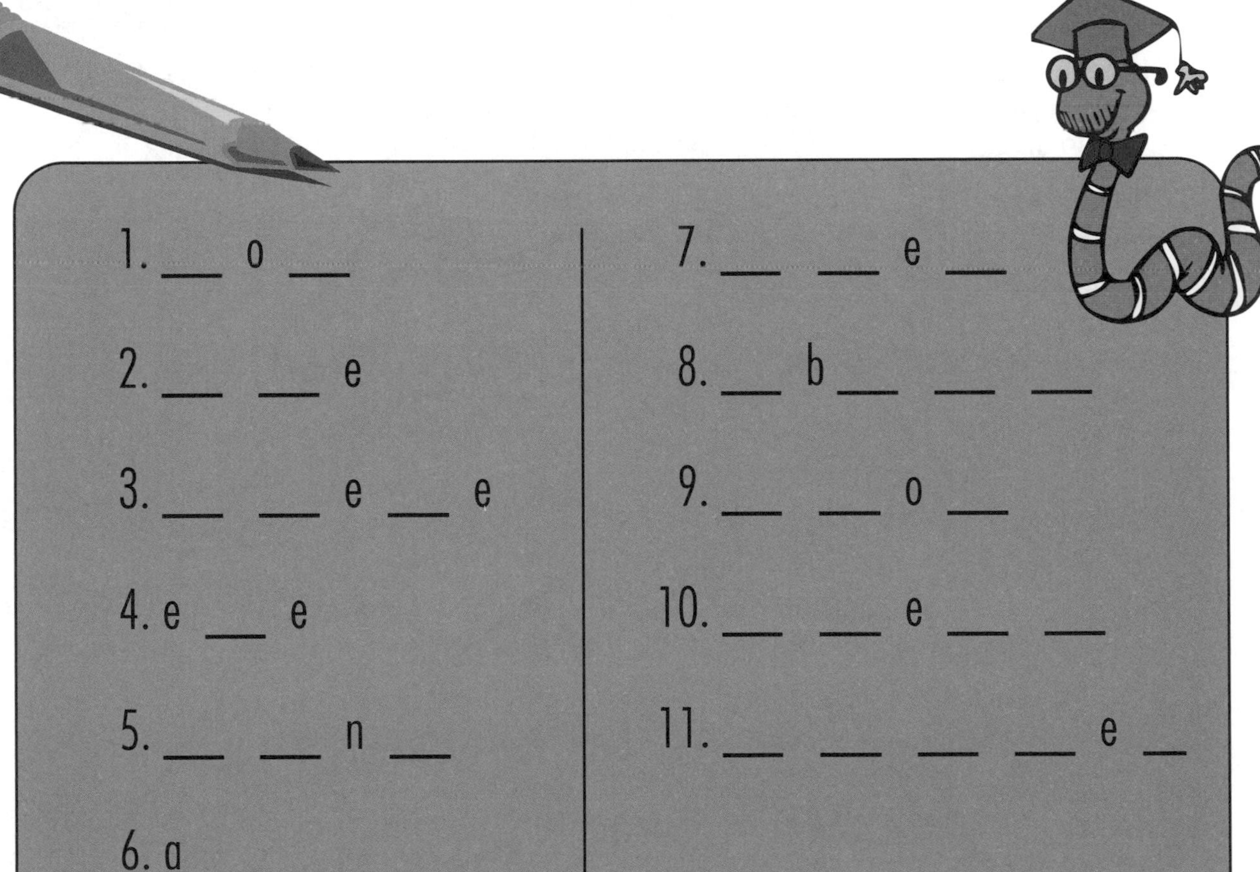

O Christmas Tree!

Decorate the Christmas tree with spelling words.

Be a word detective—look in old newspapers, magazines, and catalogs to find the words on Word List 4. Cut out at least one word for each word on the list. Glue the words on the Christmas tree. You may cut out more than one of each word, but be sure you find at least one for each word on the list.

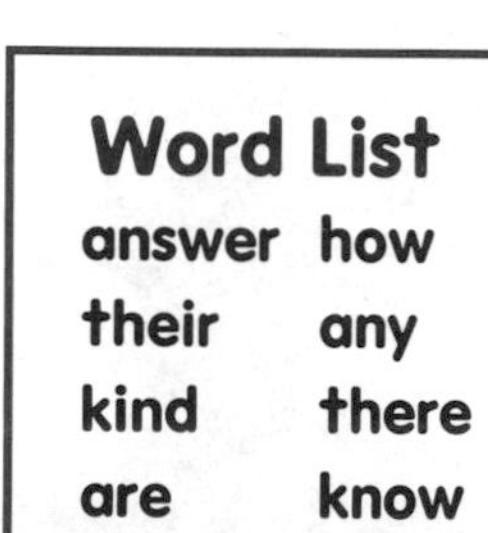

Word List

answer	how
their	any
kind	there
are	know
they	eye
about	

Colorful Candy Canes

Have fun writing the words on candy canes! Write your spelling words in red and green to form a pattern. First write the word in red crayon or colored pencil and then in green. Alternate the color until you have finished each candy cane.

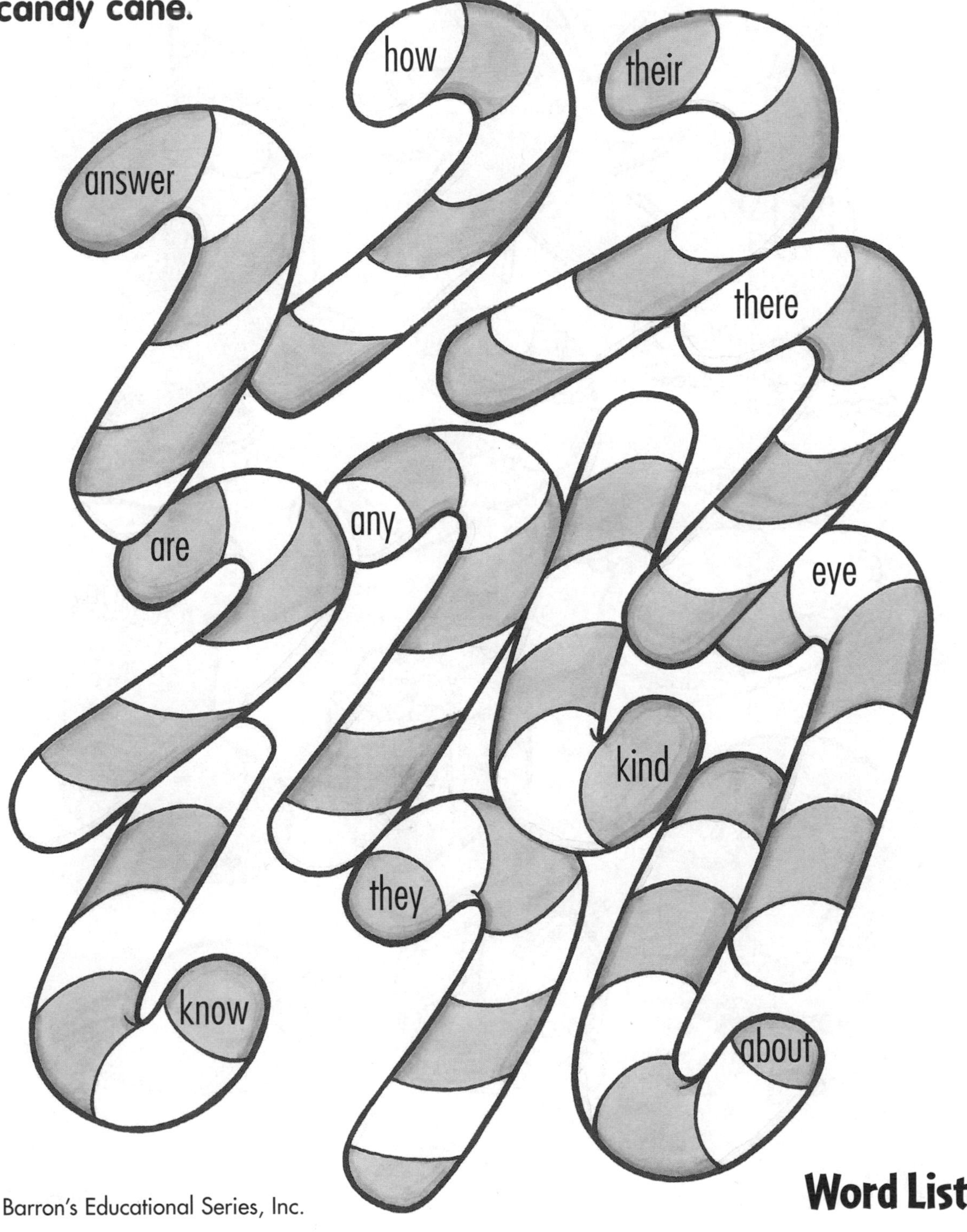

Shapes of Christmas

Write the words around each holiday shape. Write the word as many times as you can for each shape. Do your best to write small, so you can fit more words around the shape.

Happy Hanukkah!

Hanukkah is a Jewish holiday. During the celebration that lasts 8 days, a candle is lit on the menorah. Find the spelling words hidden on the menorahs. Use a yellow crayon, pencil, or marker to color each letter that builds the word.

Stocking Stuffers

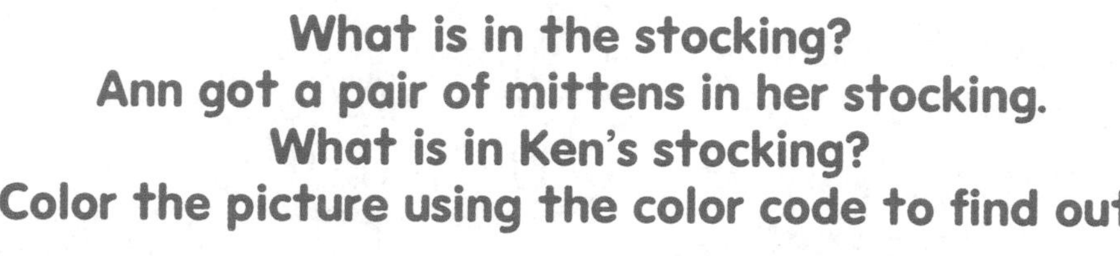

What is in the stocking?
Ann got a pair of mittens in her stocking.
What is in Ken's stocking?
Color the picture using the color code to find out.

Color Code

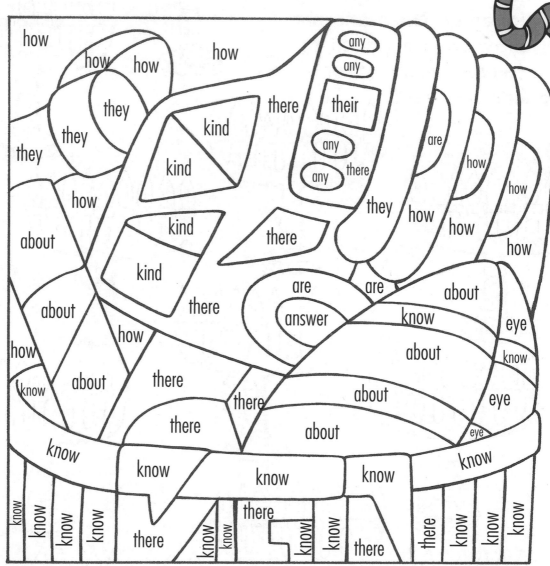

answer = orange	**any = yellow**	**are = black**	**eye = dark brown**
how = green	**kind = light blue**	**know = white**	**about = brown**
their = purple	**there = red**	**they = gray**	

Where's Rudolph?

Help Santa find Rudolph. Follow the path where all the words are spelled correctly. Use the Word List to help you.

Word List

answer	they	there
their	about	know
kind	how	eye
are	any	

Holiday Word Sort

Look at the Word List. Sort the words. Under each picture, write the spelling words with the same beginning letter as the picture.

Word List

answer	how
their	any
kind	there
are	know
they	eye
about	

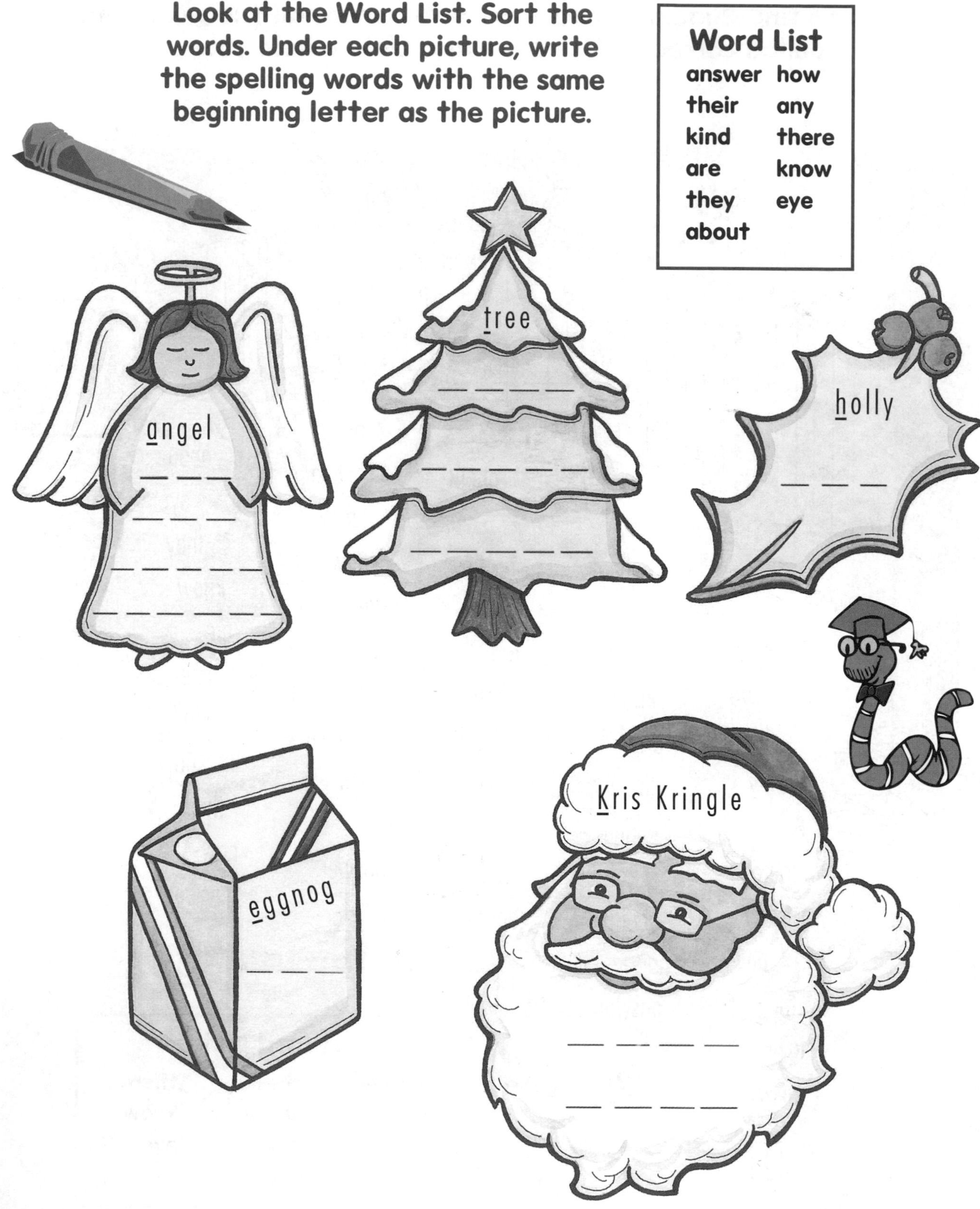

Jingle Bells!

Which of the three words matches the one on the clapper of the bell? Circle the word that matches.

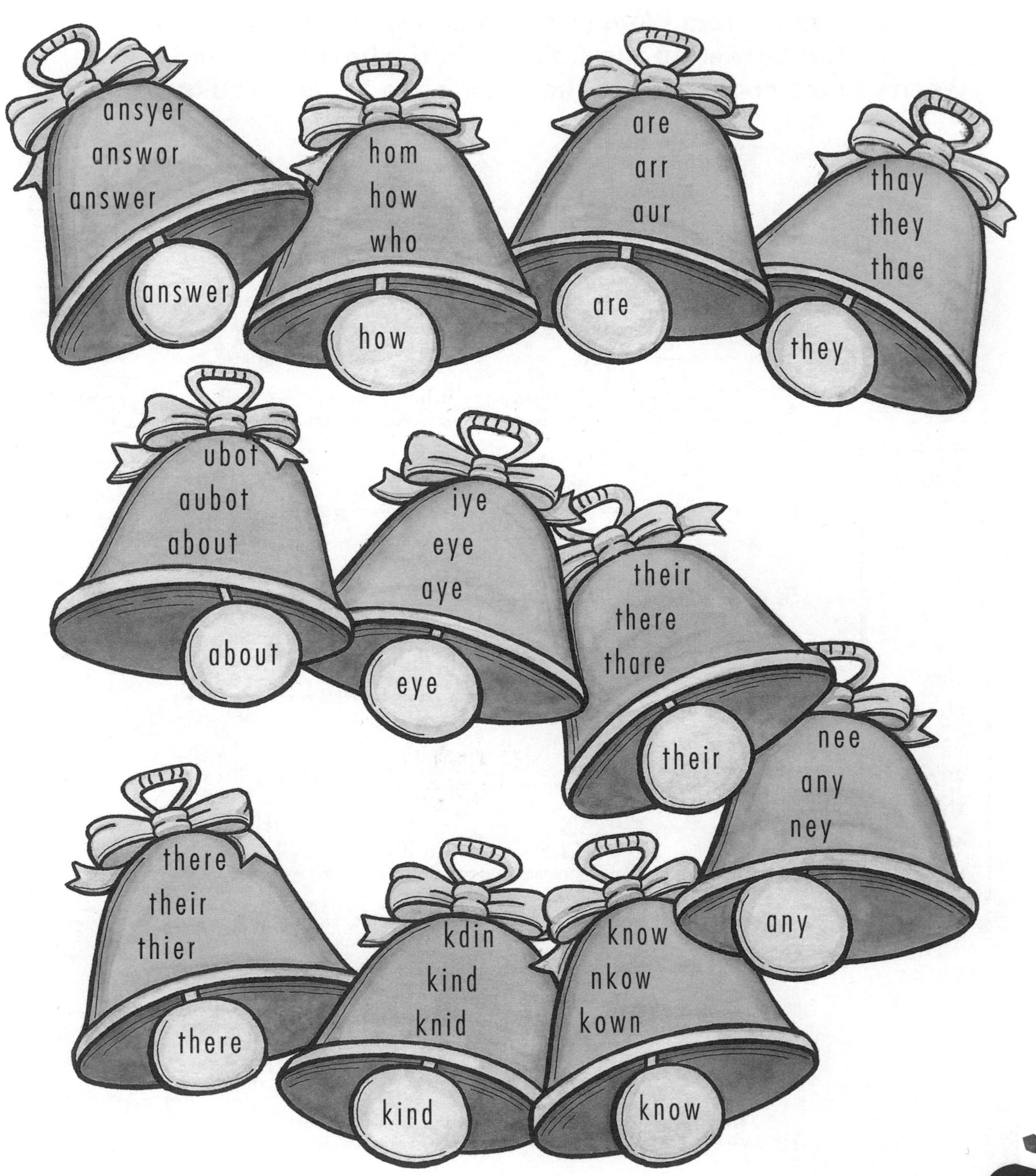

All Aboard!

Whether around your tree or used to hop on board to go visit relatives and friends, trains are a part of the holiday season. Think about the words on Word List 4. Can you spell them? Use words from Word List 4 to answer each riddle. Write the answer on the train car in the boxes provided. When you are finished, go to the facing page to see if you are correct!

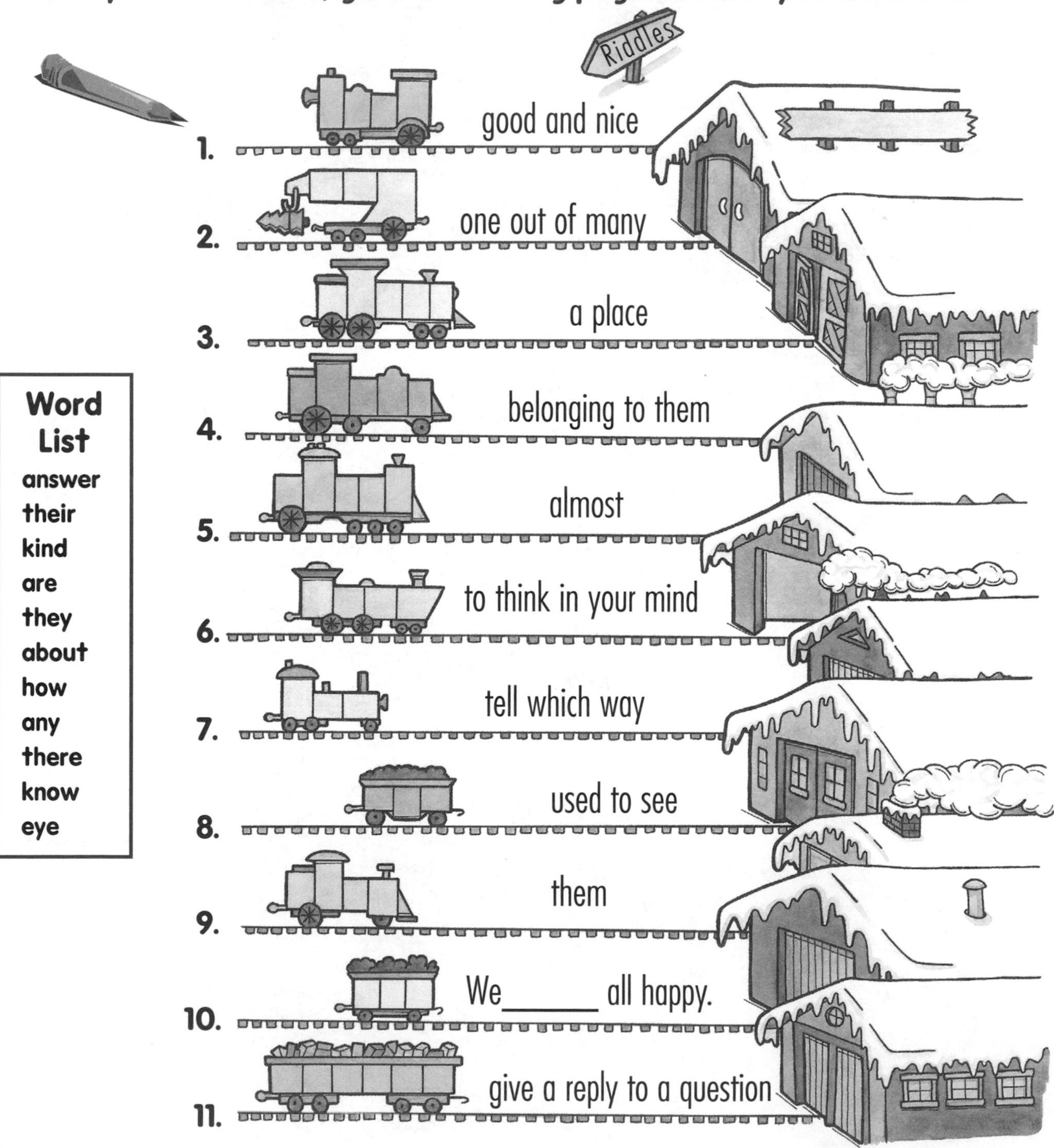

Riddles
1. good and nice
2. one out of many
3. a place
4. belonging to them
5. almost
6. to think in your mind
7. tell which way
8. used to see
9. them
10. We______ all happy.
11. give a reply to a question

Word List
- answer
- their
- kind
- are
- they
- about
- how
- any
- there
- know
- eye

Practice Time!

I hope you spelled every word correctly!

Write any misspelled words 3 times each on the lines provided.

Answers

1. kind 2. any 3. there 4. their 5. about 6. know 7. how 8. eye 9. they 10. are 11. answer

Brrr! It's January

Time to bundle up and celebrate the New Year!

Word List	
find	good
great	put
said	saw
says	school
shoes	soon

Read the word on the left. Find the word on the right that matches. Circle the picture. Be sure to look at each word carefully.

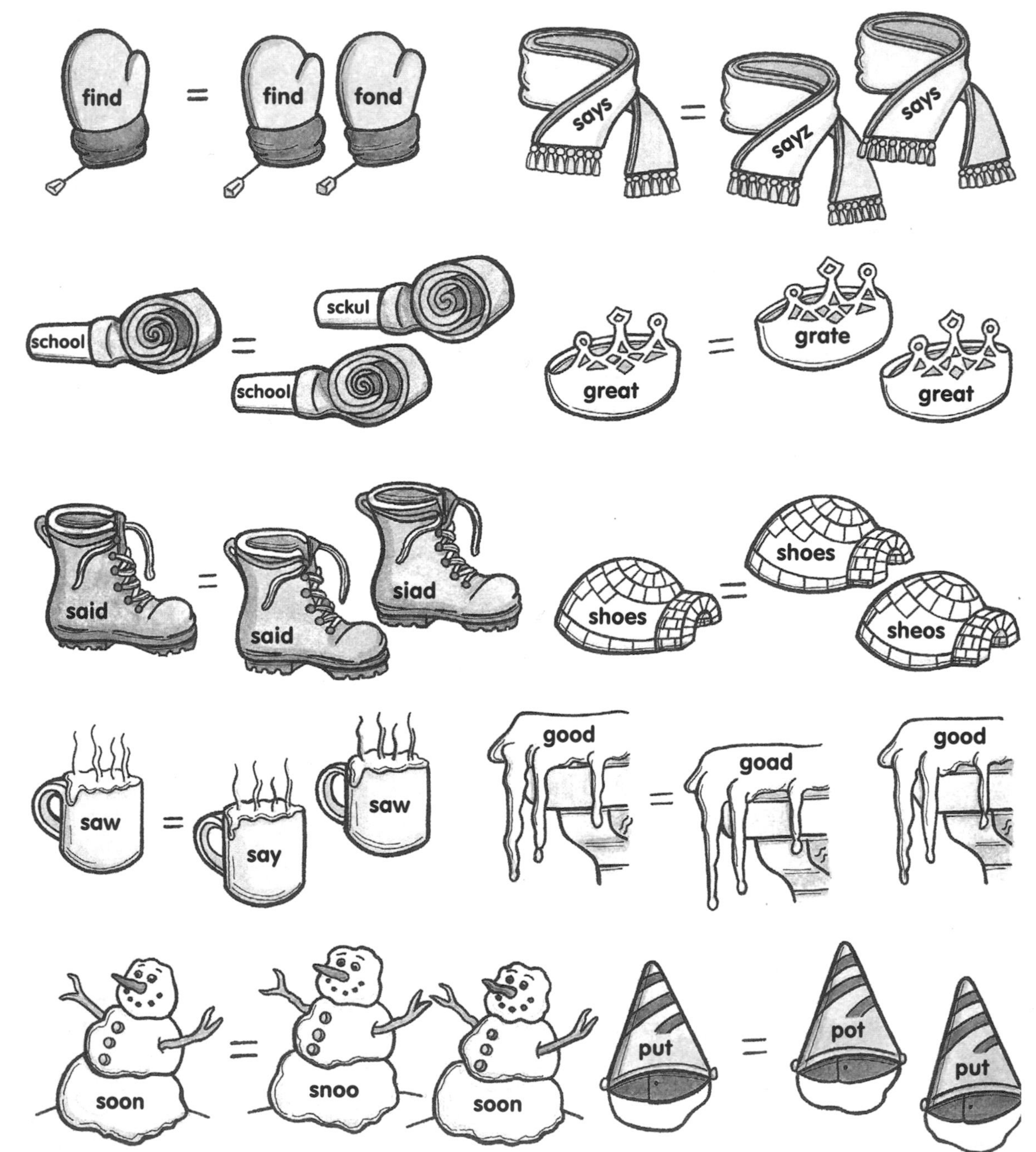

Let It Snow!!

Look at the words written in snowballs. What is the word? Use the Word List to help you. Write each word on the line.

Word List	
find	good
great	put
said	saw
says	school
shoes	soon

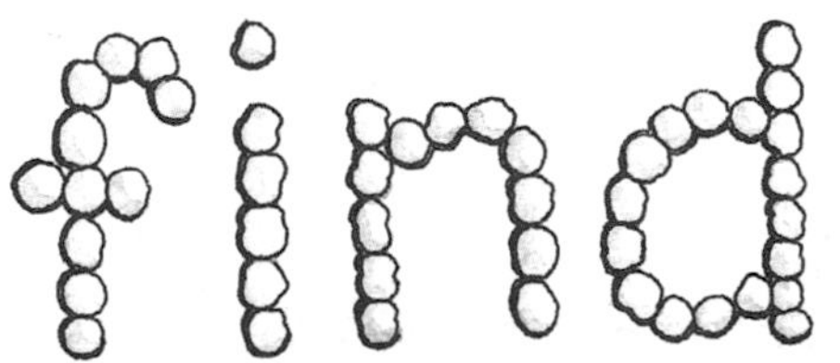

___ ___ ___ ___   ___ ___ ___ ___

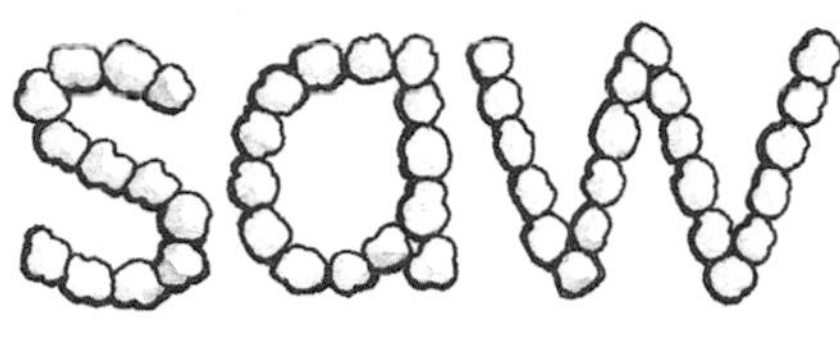

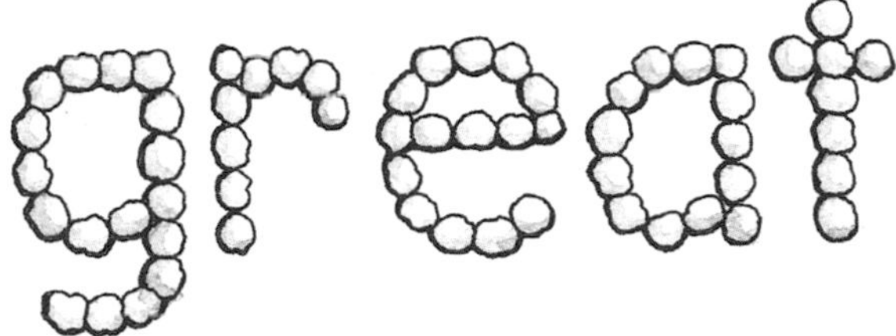

___ ___ ___   ___ ___ ___ ___ ___

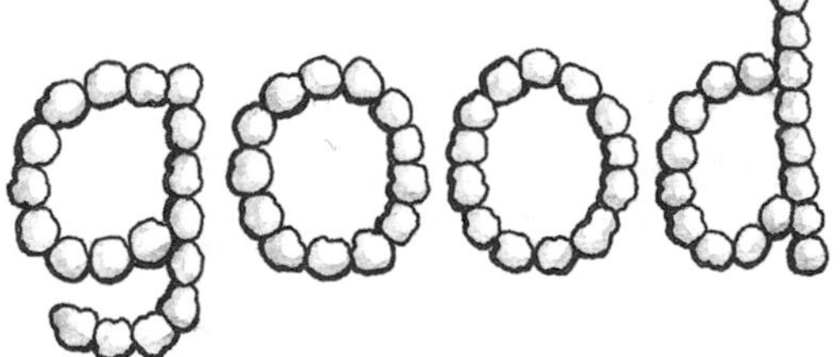

___ ___ ___ ___   ___ ___ ___ ___

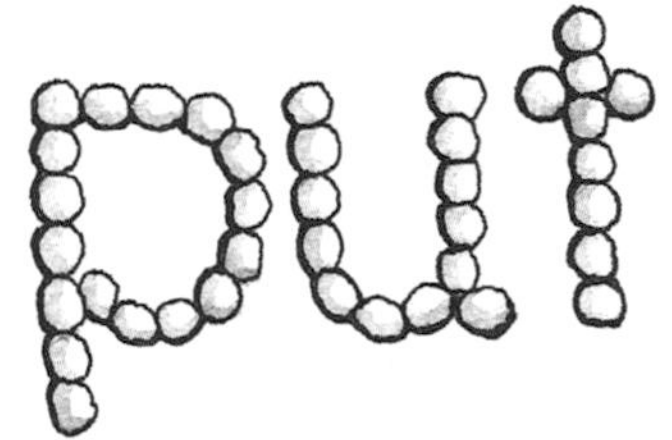

___ ___ ___ ___ ___ ___   ___ ___ ___

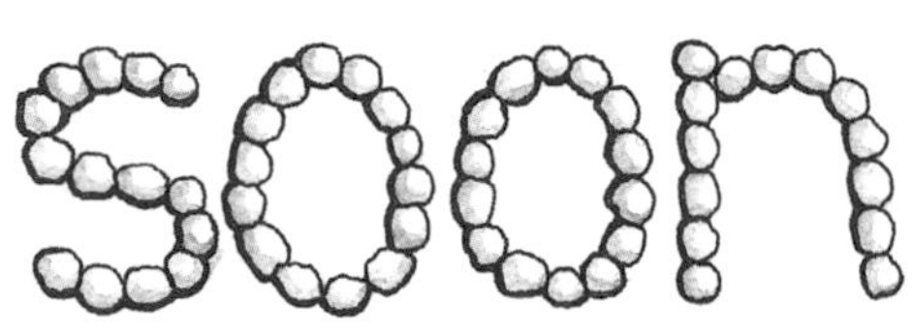

___ ___ ___ ___   ___ ___ ___ ___ ___

Nice and Warm!

Create a pretty scarf! Read the word next to the scarf. Build the word on the scarf. You may use alphabet letter stamps and an ink pad or alphabet stickers to form each word. Note: If letter stamps and ink or stickers aren't available, you may write each letter on construction paper, then cut them out. Or you may find the letters in old newspapers, catalogs, and magazines, then cut them out and glue them to build each word.

1. find
2. good
3. great
4. put
5. said
6. saw
7. says
8. school
9. shoes
10. soon

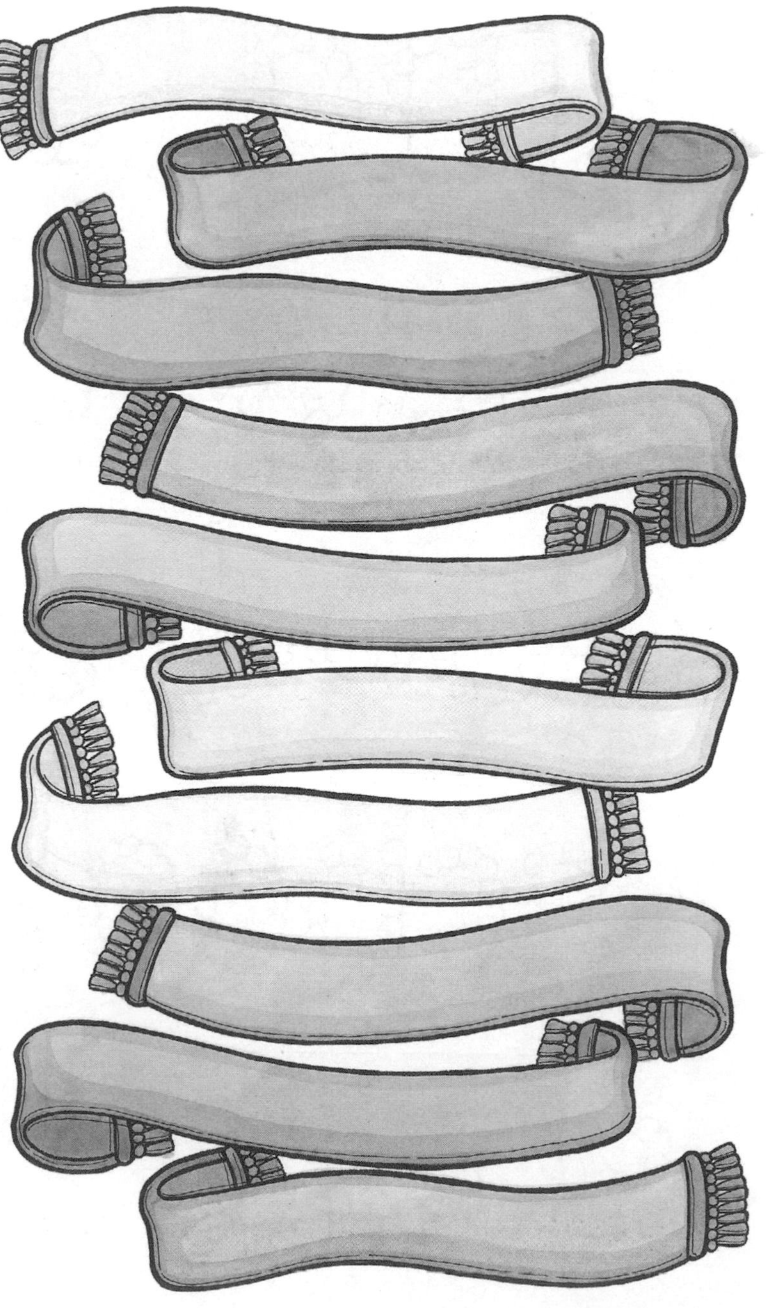

Where's My Hat?

Each snowman is missing his hat. Look at the word written on the snowman. Find the hat with the same word written on it. Draw a line from the snowman to the hat.

A Polar Wonderland!

Match the polar animal mothers to their babies. Look at the spelling word written on each polar mother. Find the mother's baby that has the spelling word spelled correctly. Color the baby to match its mother. Use the color code.

Code

- purple
- blue
- green
- orange
- red
- yellow
- black
- brown
- pink
- gray

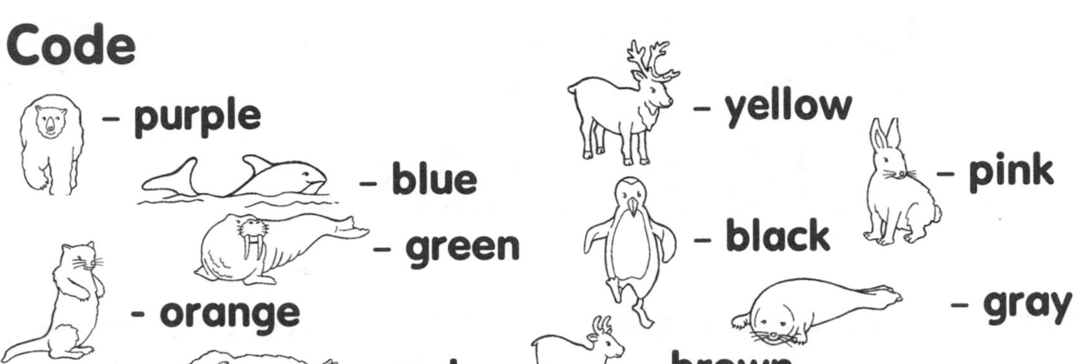

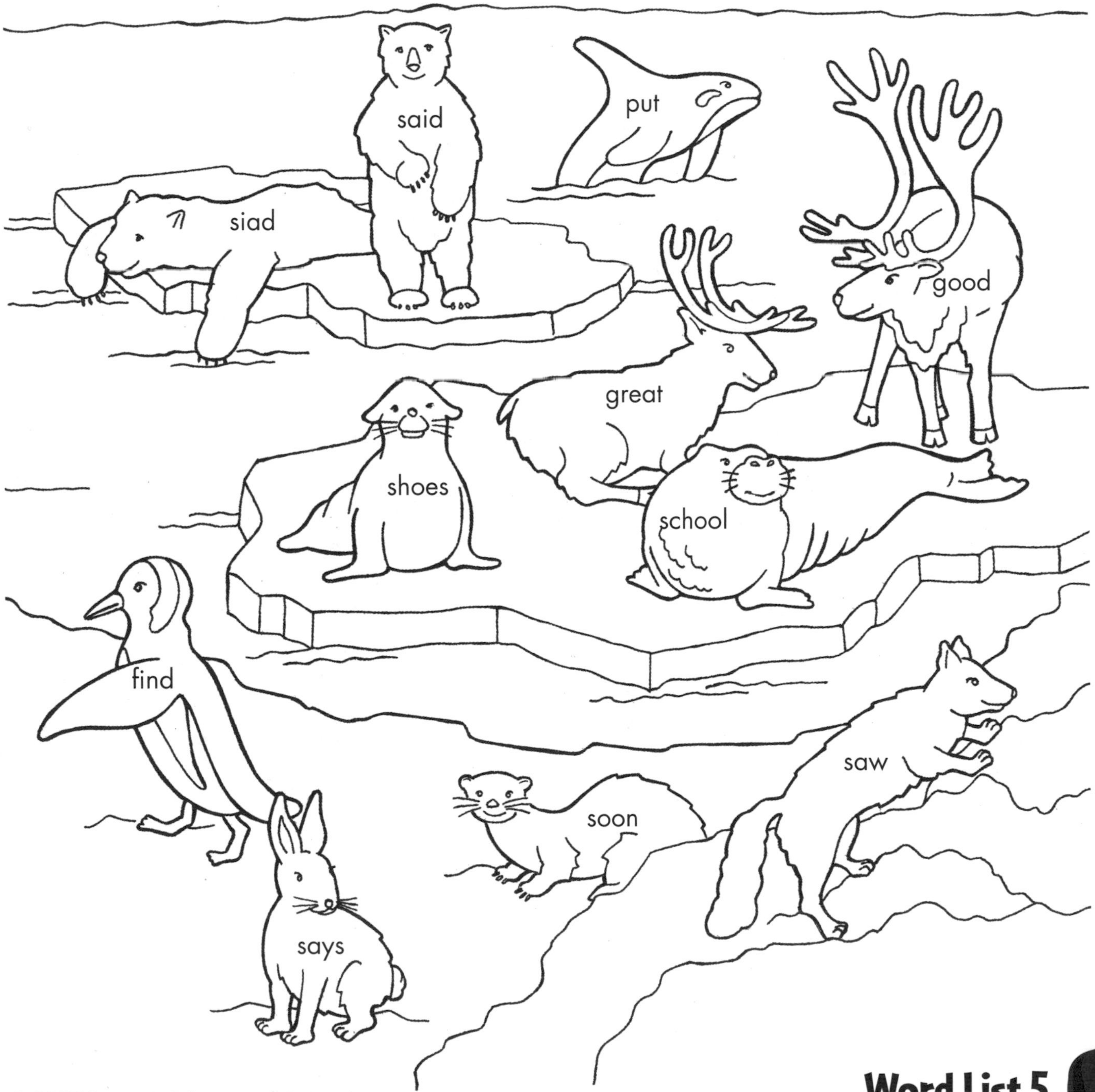

said
put
siad
good
great
shoes
school
find
saw
soon
says

Pretty Little Snowflakes

No two snowflakes are alike. Circle the word that is not the same as the one on the snowflake on the left.

Oh, What Fun!

Look at the sleds. Find the hidden spelling word or words on each sled. Circle it.

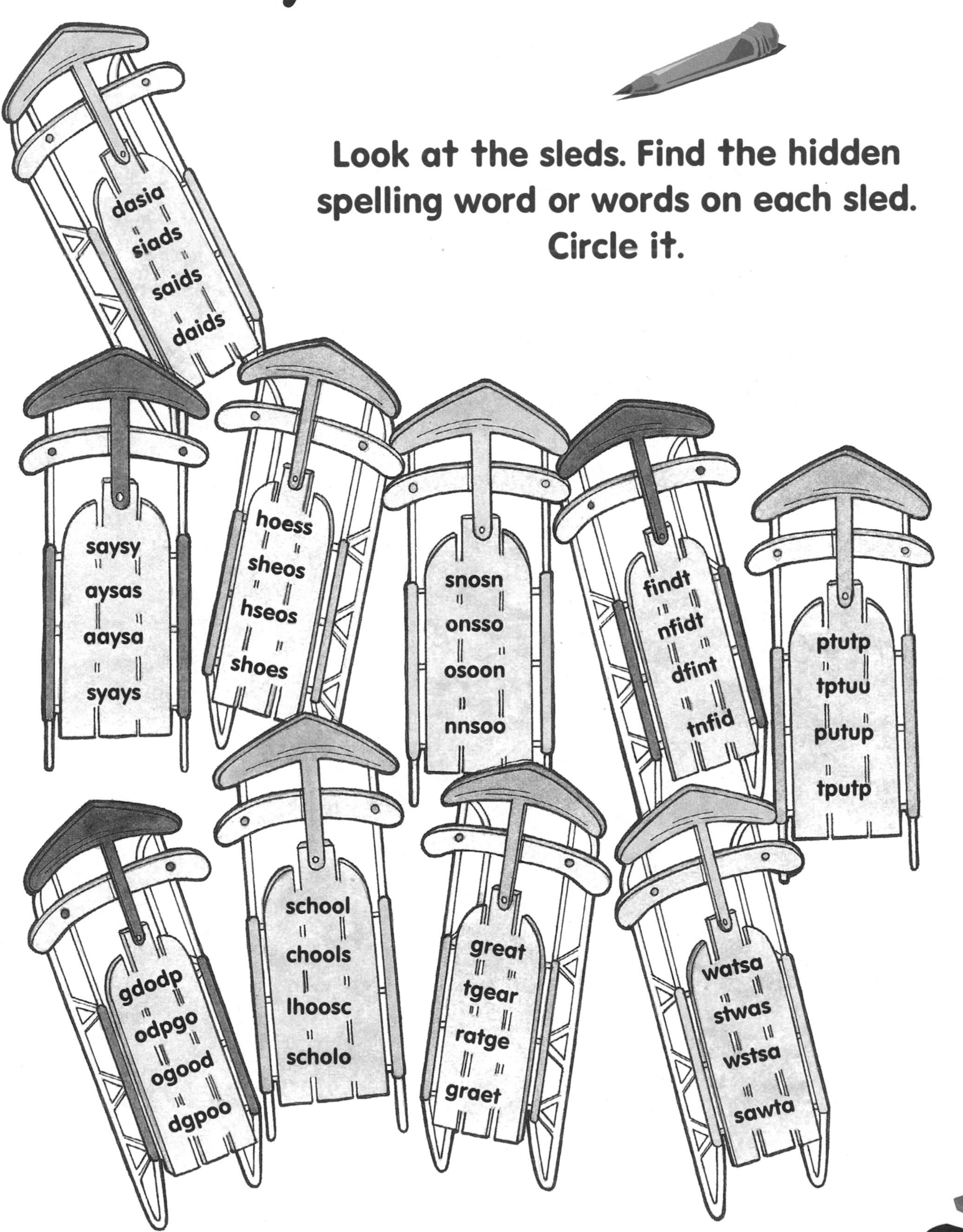

Bundle Up with Spelling!

Trace the word on the hat. Which word on the hat does not match? Circle it.

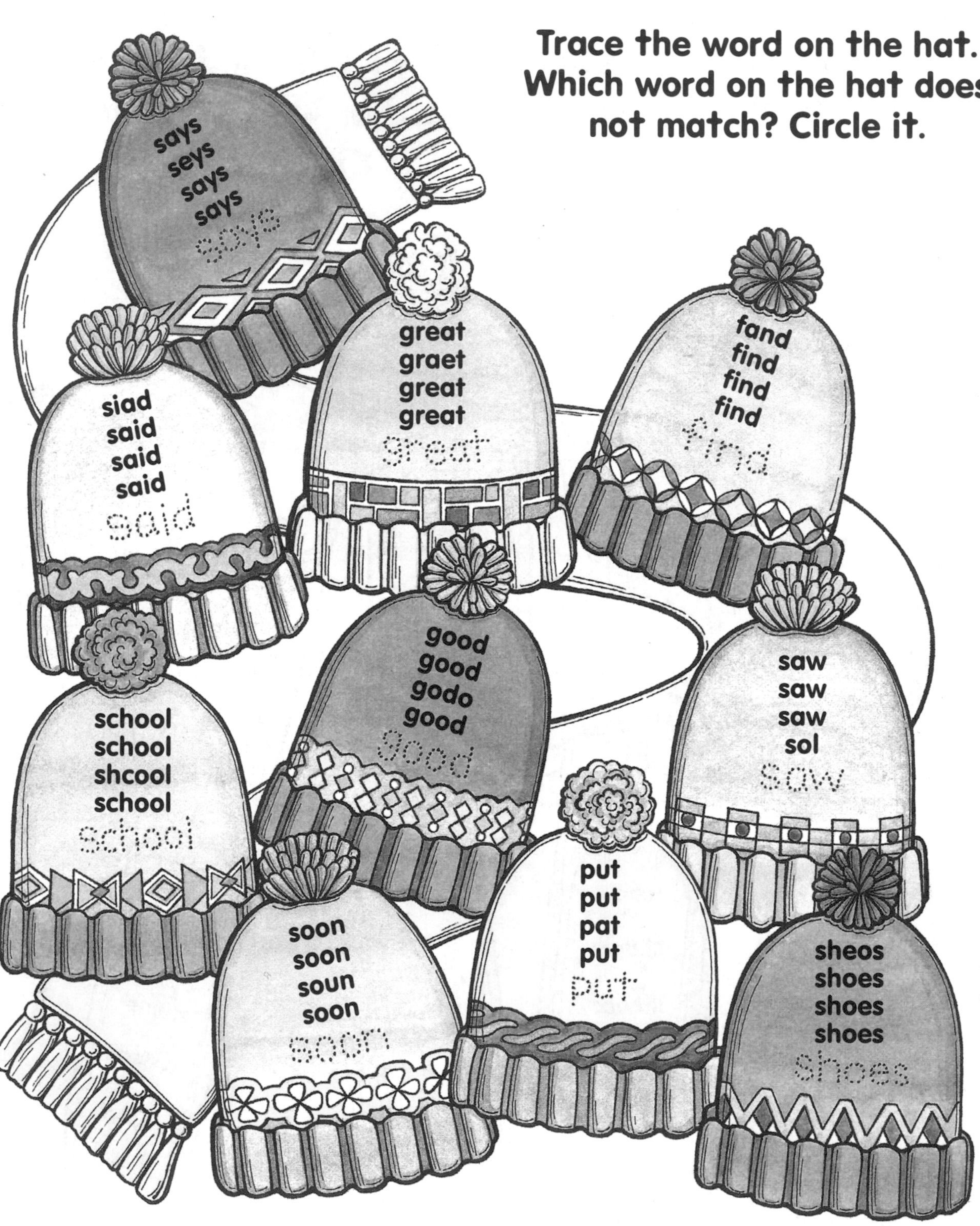

On the Wings of a Dove

Doves are a symbol of peace. In January we remember that Dr. Martin Luther King, Jr. wanted peaceful change.

Look at the doves. Fill in the missing letters.

Dr. Martin Luther King, Jr. ______, "I have a dream...."

Circle the dove that has the word on it that fills in the blank.

Showtime!

Time to show what you know. Think of the words you have been working on in this practice set. Write the spelling word that answers each riddle.

1. before long, in a short time ____________________
2. a place to learn ____________________
3. past form of see ____________________
4. Fill in the missing letters to form the word that belongs in the blank.

   Jan __ __ ys, "Let's skate!"
5. A word that rhymes with *crate* that means you did a good job.

   ____
6. You wear them on your feet. ____________________
7. to place ____________________
8. to look for and get ____________________
9. This cake tastes ____________________. It is yummy.
10. Fill in the missing letters. The coach s___ ___d, "It is time for skating lessons."

Answers on the following page.

I hope you spelled every word correctly!

Write any misspelled words 3 times each on the lines provided.

Answers

1. soon 2. school 3. saw 4. sa 5. great 6. shoes 7. put 8. find 9. good 10. ai

Groundhog Spelling Math

Answer these problems.

1. m + brother – br = ____________________
2. buy – u = ____________________
3. b + muy – m = ____________________
4. mother – ther + ve = ____________________
5. want – nt + s = ____________________
6. watch – wat – h + ircle = ____________________
7. br + mother – m = ____________________
8. was – s + nt = ____________________

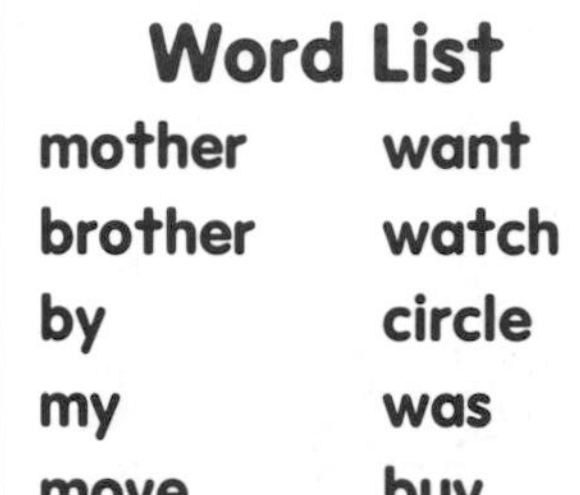

Word List

mother	want
brother	watch
by	circle
my	was
move	buy

Groundhog Facts

groundhog + shadow = winter
groundhog – shadow = spring

Heart to Heart Spelling

Build each spelling word on the hearts. Cut letters from old magazines, newspapers, and catalogs. Glue each letter to form the spelling word or use alphabet stickers, peeling and sticking letters to build each word. Note: If you run out of a certain sticker letter, cut the letter out of an old magazine, catalog, or newspaper and glue it on.

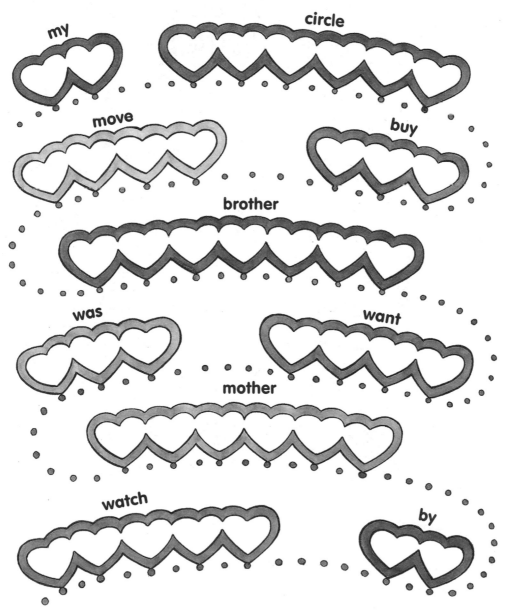

my

circle

move

buy

brother

was

want

mother

watch

by

Who's Who? What's What?

Unscramble the words on each president's profile.

1. ________________
2. ________________
3. ________________
4. ________________
5. ________________

1. ecilrc
2. thacw
3. yb
4. aws
5. tawn

1. ym
2. hremot
3. trebohr
4. vemo
5. yub

1. ________________
2. ________________
3. ________________
4. ________________
5. ________________

George Washington and Abraham Lincoln were presidents of the United States. They were both born in February.

A Priceless Gift!

Edit a story. Circle the words that are spelled wrong. Then write them correctly on the lines below.

The Gift

I wont to bey my muther a gift for Valentine's Day. I think she would like a wutch. A watch costs a lot. I will ask mi big bruther to help me buy a watch for Mother. My brother has a job. He will help me buy a gift. Mother will be happy with her gift. But she will be even more pleased that we went together to get it.

1. ____________________

2. ____________________

3. ____________________

4. ____________________

5. ____________________

6. ____________________

We love you, Mom!

Code Jewels

Look at each necklace. Look at the code. Use the code to write the correct spelling word on each bead.

Crack the code! Write the word for each shape on the jewel of each necklace.

What is the pattern?
Write the word pattern.

____

What is the pattern?
Write the word pattern.

____

Code

move =  watch =  was =  by =

Get to the Heart of It!

**Fill in the answers to the puzzle.
Use the Word List to help you.**

Word List	
mother	want
brother	watch
by	circle
my	was
move	buy

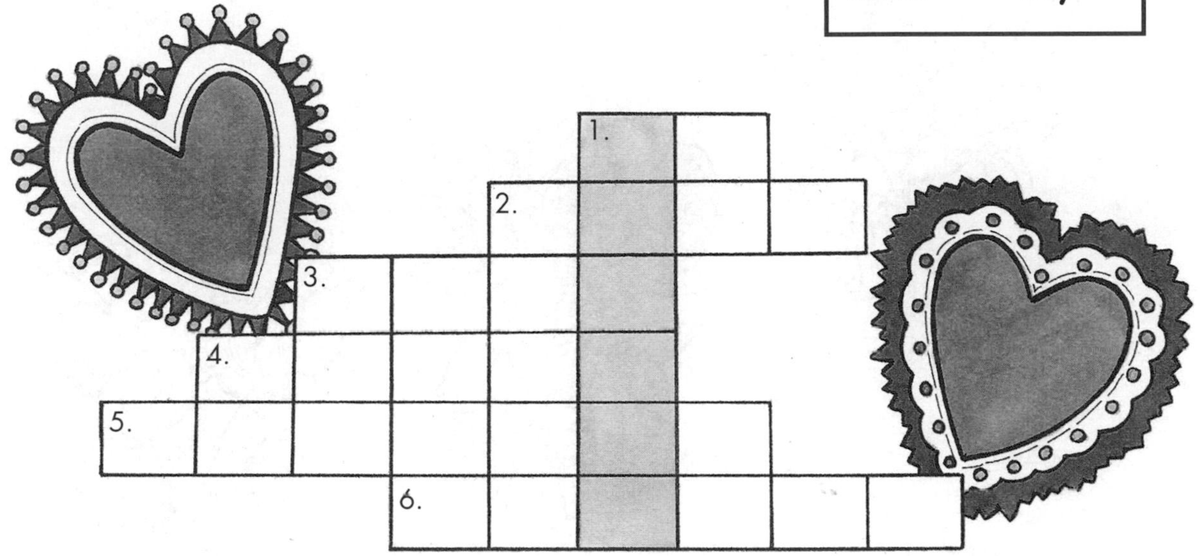

1. belonging to me
2. to change position
3. to wish for
4. to look at
5. a boy family member
6. a shape

Now look at the shaded box in each answer. Put the letters in each shaded box together to make a spelling word that fills in the blank. Write the word on the line below.

I love my ______________________________ .

Rosy Endings

Sort the spelling words by ending letter. Write the words that end with the letter written on the rose.

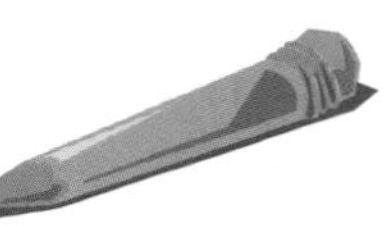

r r r

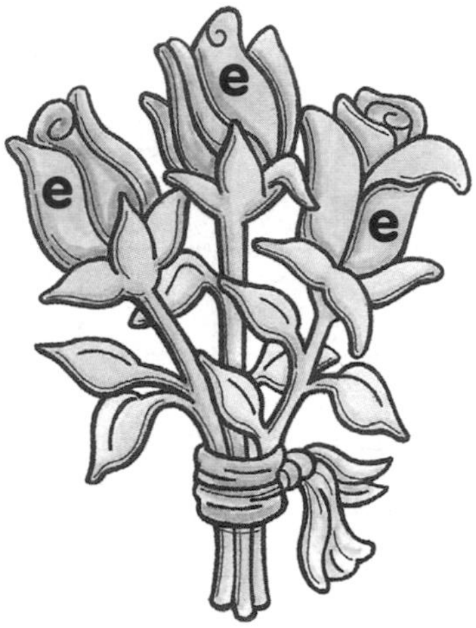

e e e

t t t

y y y

s s s

h h h

Which Way to the Tarts?

Help the Queen of Hearts find her tarts!

Follow the path where all the words are spelled correctly. Use the Word List to help you.

Word List	
mother	want
brother	watch
by	circle
my	was
move	buy

1. brother
mother
was
circle
want
watch
by
my
buy
move

2. brother
want
move
my
muther
by
circle
watch
was
buy

3. brother
buy
move
by
whatch
mother
want
was
my
circal

Take Aim at Spelling

Find the hidden spelling words on cupid's arrows.

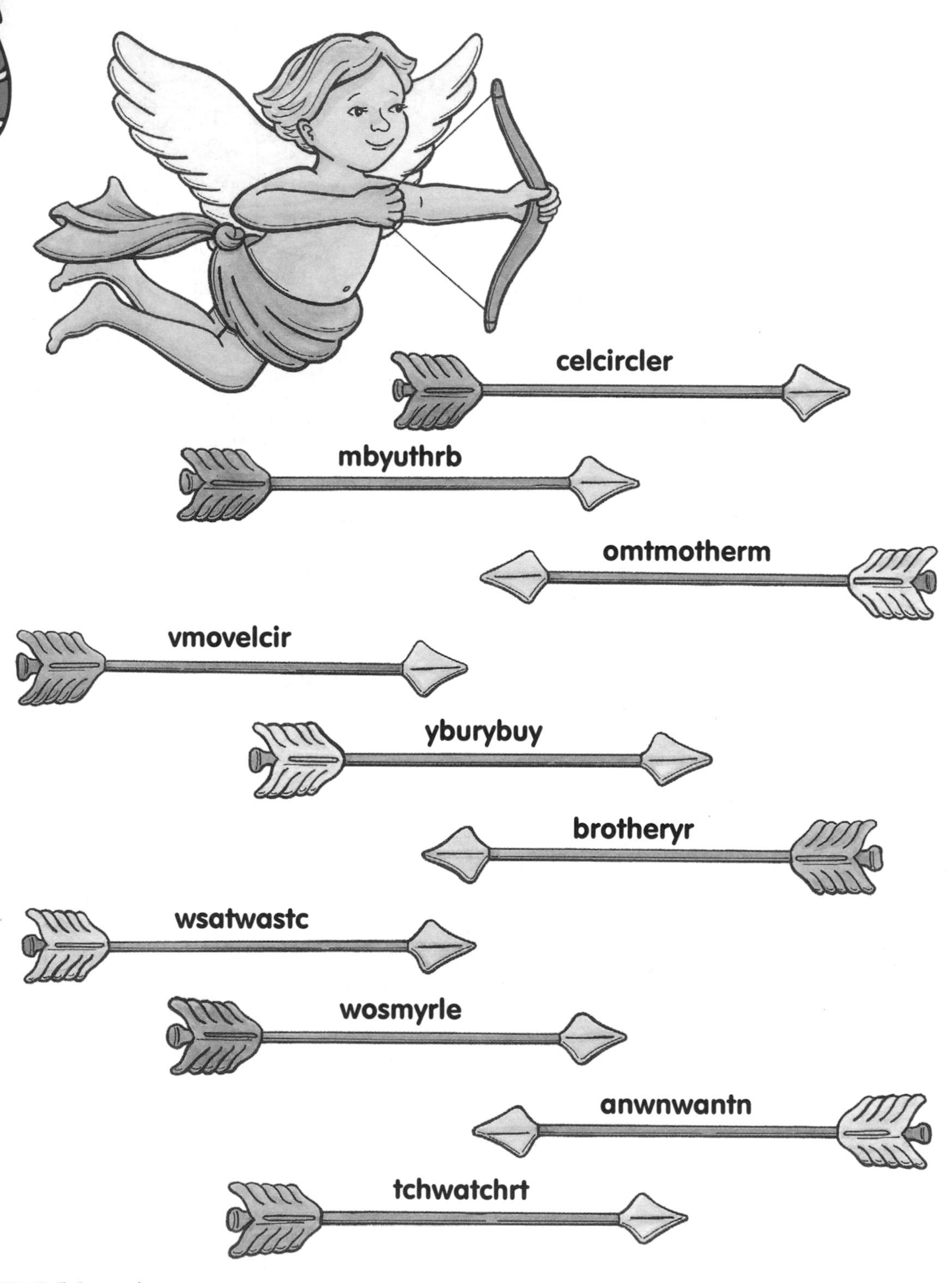

Put Your Heart Into Spelling

Can you spell the words on List 6?

1. a boy with a sister
   b __ o __ h __ __
2. get up and go
   m __ __ e
3. a word for mom
   __ __ t __ e __
4. belongs to me
   m __
5. near
   b __
6. at some point in time
   w __ s
7. a shape
   c __ r __ l __
8. to spend money on
   __ __ y
9. to think of and wish for
   __ __ nt
10. to look at
    w __ t __ h

Answers on the following page.

I hope you spelled every word correctly!

Write any misspelled words 3 times each on the lines provided.

Answers

1. brother 2. move 3. mother 4. my 5. by 6. was 7. circle 8. buy 9. want 10. watch

Lions or Lambs?

March is said to come in like a lion and go out like a lamb. This means that the weather is like winter early in March, but often by the end of the month the weather gets better, showing all that spring is on the way.

Word List

as	laugh
to	away
lion	too
food	look
took	ball

Look at the words. Some are spelled correctly, and some are not. Put the misspelled words on the lion side, and put the correct words on the lamb side.

away lok took to as
liun ball toi laf food

Up and Away!

March winds make kites fly. How many correct kites do you spy?

Color the kites that have the word spelled correctly. How many did you find?

____

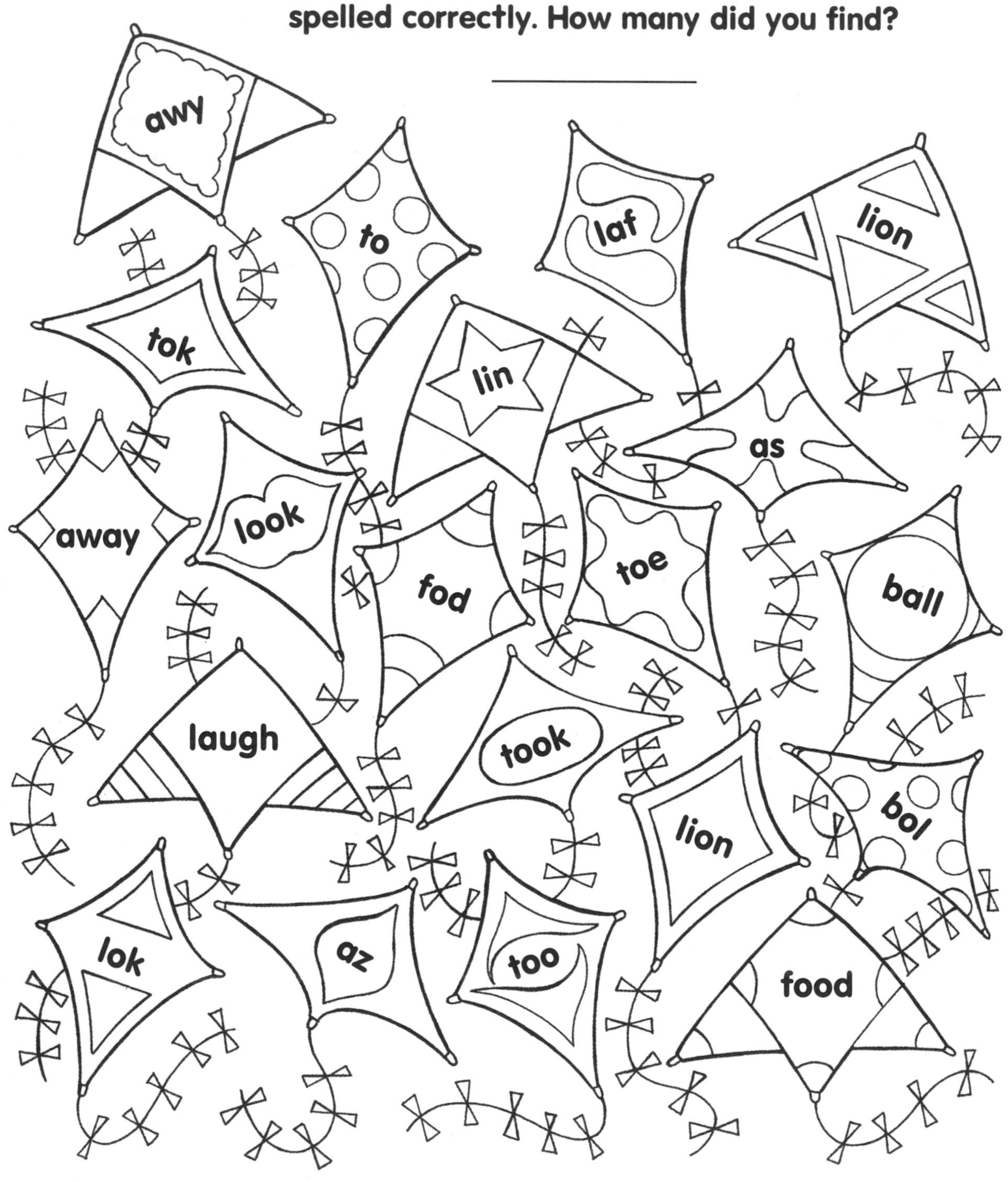

Where's Me Pots of Gold?

Help the leprechaun find his pots of gold. Match the pieces of the pot to build a spelling word.

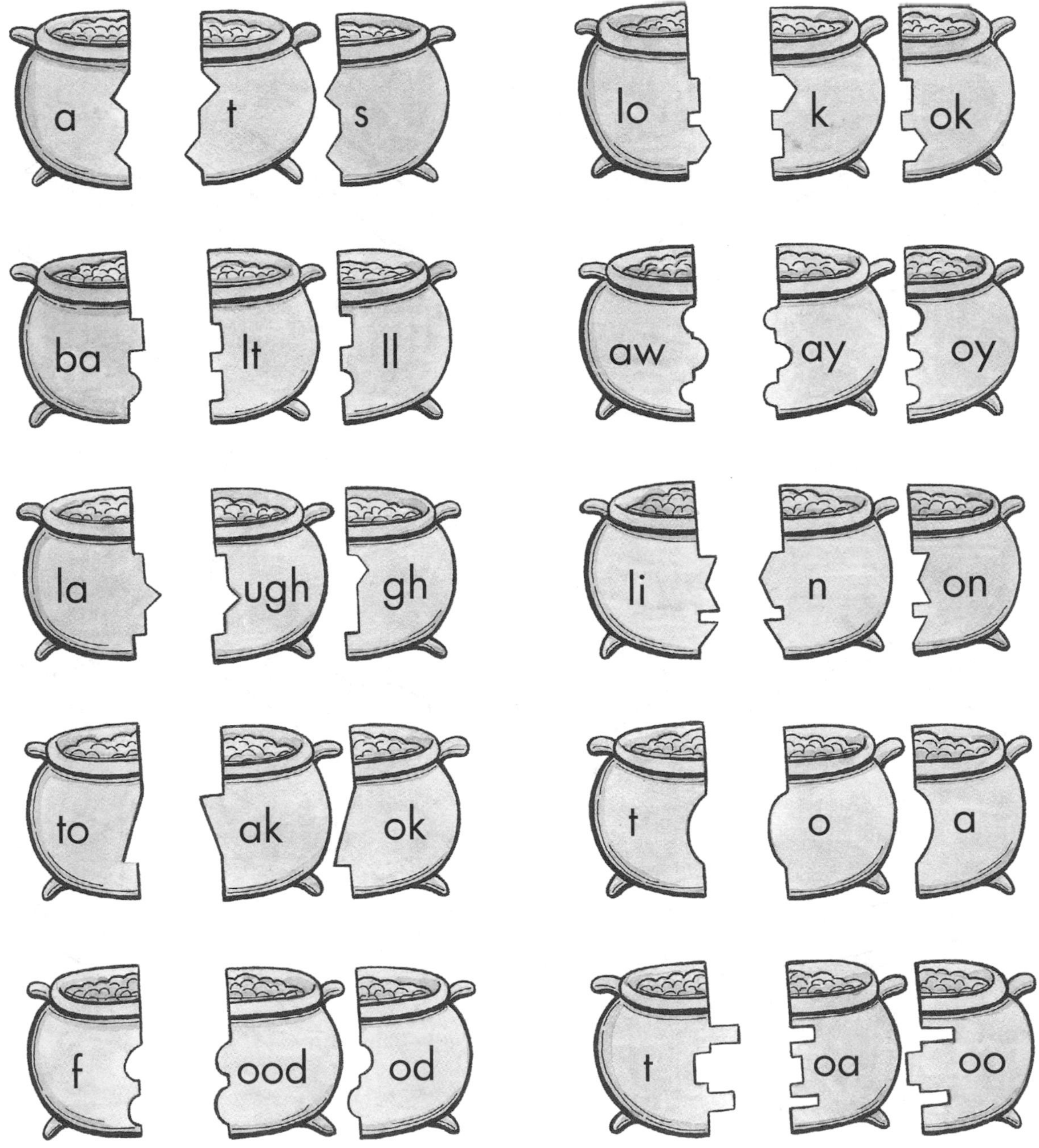

Word Rainbows

A rainbow is made up of these colors:
red, orange, yellow, green, blue, indigo blue-purple, violet-purple

The first letter of each color forms a man's name: Roy G Biv. Remember the name Roy G Biv, and you will always know the colors of the rainbow.

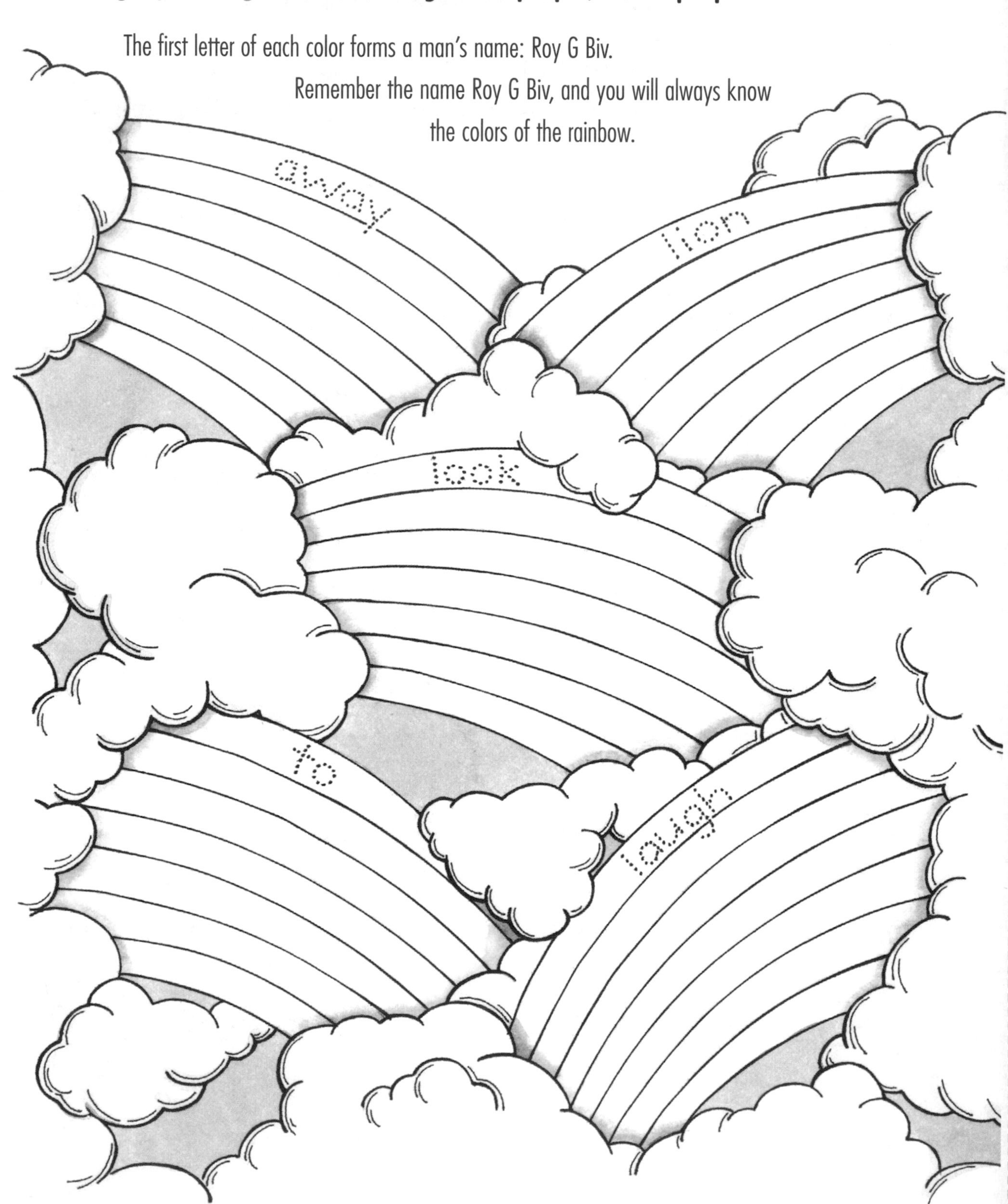

Trace each word in red. Use any writing tool you wish: colored pencil, marker, pen, or crayon. After you trace the word in red, then write the word in each of the colors of the rainbow. When you have written the word in orange, yellow, green, blue, indigo blue-purple, and violet-purple, then color, paint, or use colored pencils to color the rainbow as marked. Be sure that you can still see the words you've written. Note: Do not use marker to color your rainbow; it will hide the words you've written.

No Blarney!

The shamrock is a plant with three bright green leaves. It is the national emblem of Ireland.

Print the spelling word on the lines around each shamrock.

Oh, What a Parade!

Let's get in order.

These 10 people are marching in the St. Patrick's Day parade. Use the code to write the correct spelling word on the sash for each person in the line.

What Luck!

Read the story. Circle all the spelling words you can find. Don't let any get away! Be sure to catch all 7.

Lucky Leprechaun

I tried to catch a leprechaun, so I hid behind a tree. When he ran by, I reached out to grab him, but in a flash and with a laugh he dashed away. I don't know how it happened, because as I grabbed at him, I felt I had him good, but when I took a closer look, all I had was his little green coat. What luck!

St. Patrick's Day Surprise!

Use the code to fill in the blanks. Who is in the parade?

Parade Surprise

Boom! Boom! went the drums in the band, and music filled the air. "1. ________," said Dad while standing at the door. "The St. Patrick's Day parade has just begun."

I ran 2. ________ 3. ________ out the window.

I saw people standing in a line. They were looking hard at something, and they began to 4. ________. Then I saw it, 5. ________. It was a cute little doggie decked out in green with a green 6. ________ in his mouth.

What an Irish surprise!

Code

ball =

look =

too =

laugh =

took =

to =

1. ________
2. ________
3. ________
4. ________
5. ________
6. ________

Derby Daze

Which of the derby hats have misspelled words on them? Circle them, then write the words correctly on the lines below.

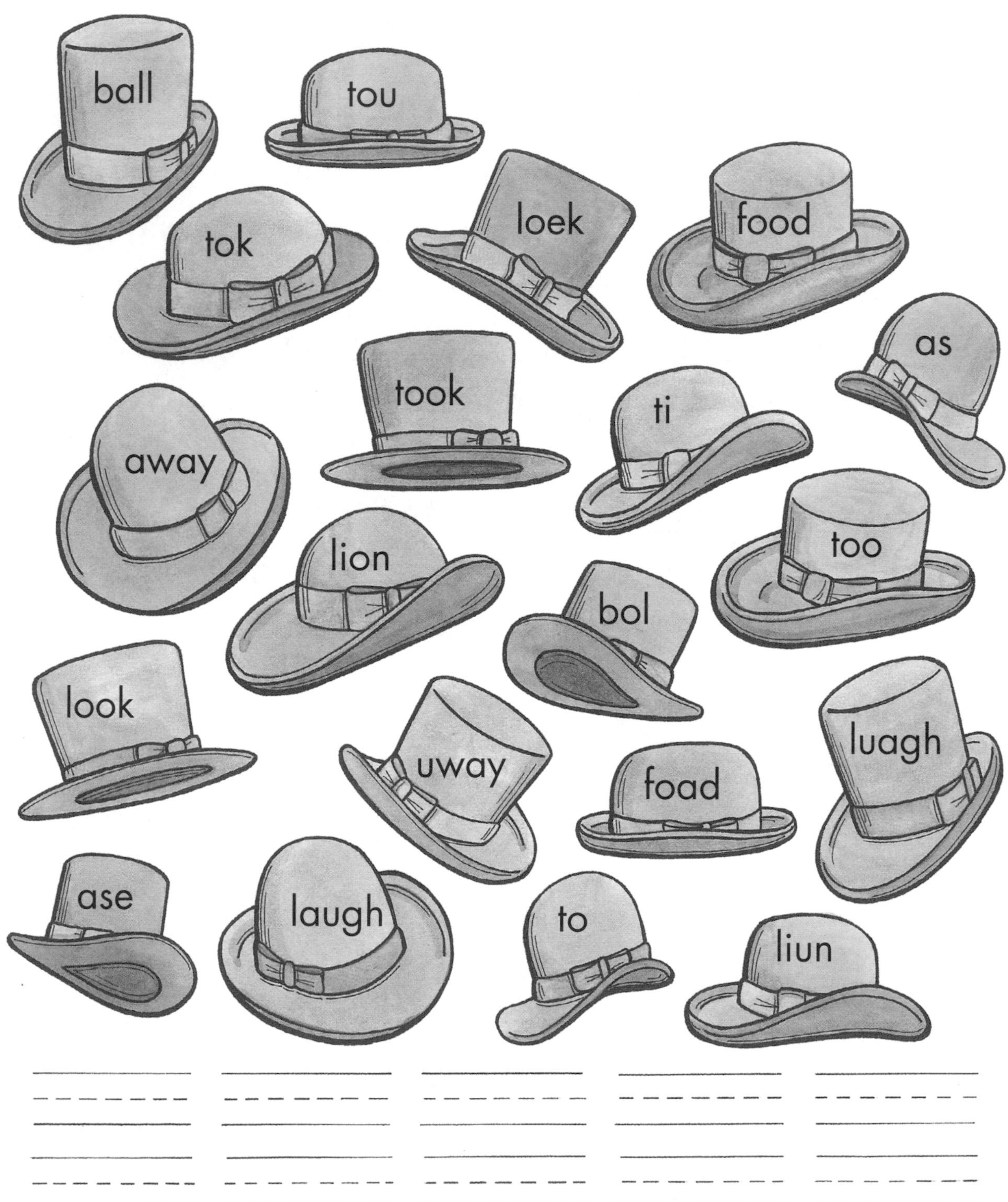

A Lucky Kiss!

What do you know?

Think of each spelling word in this practice set. Use a spelling word from Word List 7 to answer each riddle. Write the spelling word on the line. When you are finished, go to the following page to see if you are correct.

Do you know that you can go to Blarney Castle, in Ireland, and kiss the Blarney Stone? It is said that if you kiss the Blarney Stone, you are given the gift of eloquent speech. That means you speak in a very pleasing way.

1. ha, ha ____________

2. ________________ is something we eat.

3. A _______________ is a toy that can bounce.

4. _________________ means to see.

5. A _________________ is a jungle animal.

6. far ________________

7. also _______________

8. I _________________ a nap.

9. I tripped __________ I ran.

10. I want ____________ catch a leprechaun.

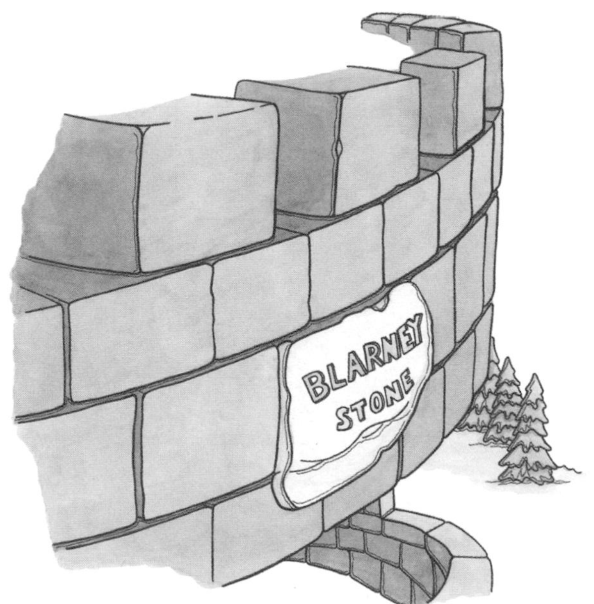

Answers on the following page.

I hope you spelled every word correctly!

Write any misspelled words 3 times each on the lines provided.

____________	____________	____________
____________	____________	____________
____________	____________	____________
____________	____________	____________
____________	____________	____________
____________	____________	____________
____________	____________	____________
____________	____________	____________
____________	____________	____________
____________	____________	____________
____________	____________	____________

Answers

1. laugh 2. Food 3. Ball 4. Look 5. lion 6. away 7. too 8. took 9. as 10. to

Umbrella Time!

Trace the word, and then fill in the missing letter. When you are finished, write the whole word in the blank spaces. Use the Word List to help you.

Word List

do	oh
where	does
of	who
down	old
won	one

Egg Hunt

Help Kim and Tom find the hidden eggs. Circle the eggs you find. Then if the word on the egg is spelled incorrectly, rewrite it correctly on the Easter basket below.

one

ald

whu

ov

wone

wun

of

do

oo

does

dose

oh

doun

du

whear

where

down

won

who

old

1. 2. 3.

4. 5. 6. 7.

8. 9. 10.

Colored Eggs

Color the eggs!
Follow the code.

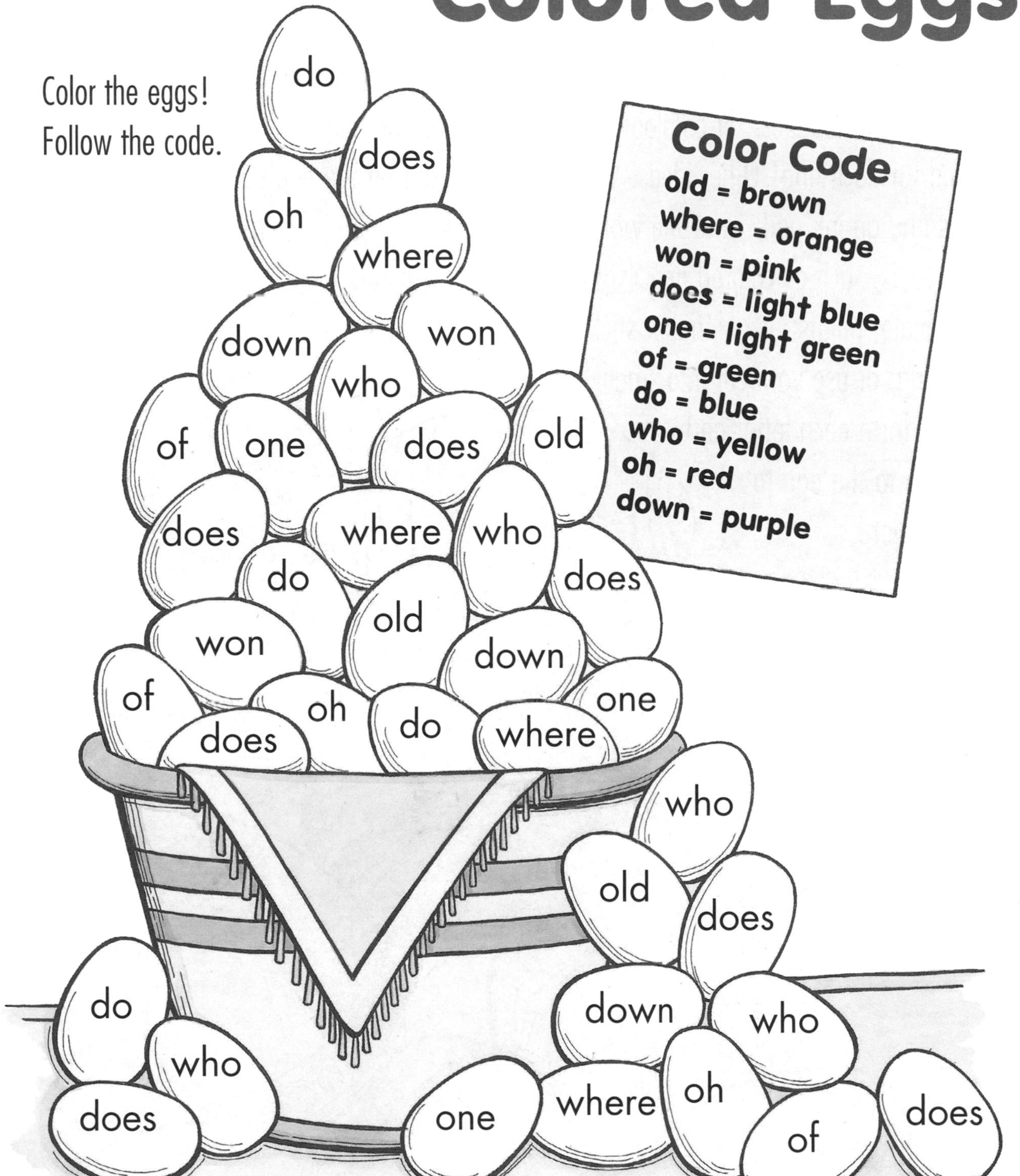

Color Code

old = brown
where = orange
won = pink
does = light blue
one = light green
of = green
do = blue
who = yellow
oh = red
down = purple

do
does
oh
where
down
won
who
of
one
does
old
does
where
who
do
does
old
won
down
of
oh
do
where
one
does
who
old
does
do
down
who
who
does
one
where
oh
of
does

Which color was used the most? Look at the Color Code.
Write the word for that color. ______________________

Amazing Eggs!

Decorate the Easter eggs with the words from the Word List. You may cut the word from old magazines, newspapers, or catalogs and glue them on the egg. See how many words you can find for each one! Other ideas: Stamp the word out on the egg using alphabet letter stamps and an ink pad; write the word over and over on the egg using different colors and writing tools, such as colored pencils, pens, markers, crayons, or watercolor paints; use alphabet stickers to build the word on the egg; or use yarn cut into small pieces to form each letter and glue them to the egg to build the word.

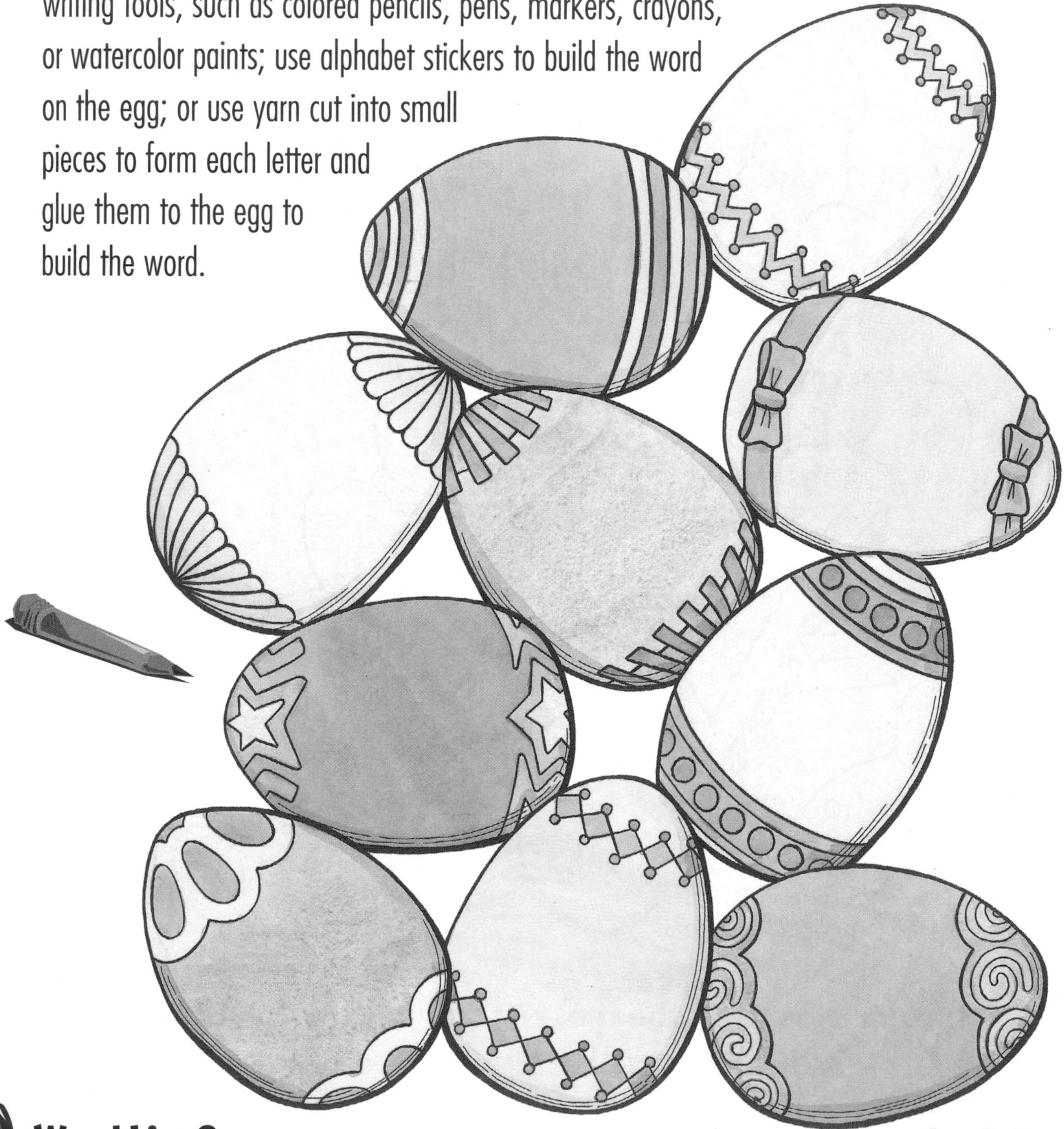

Word List

do	oh
where	does
of	who
down	old
won	one

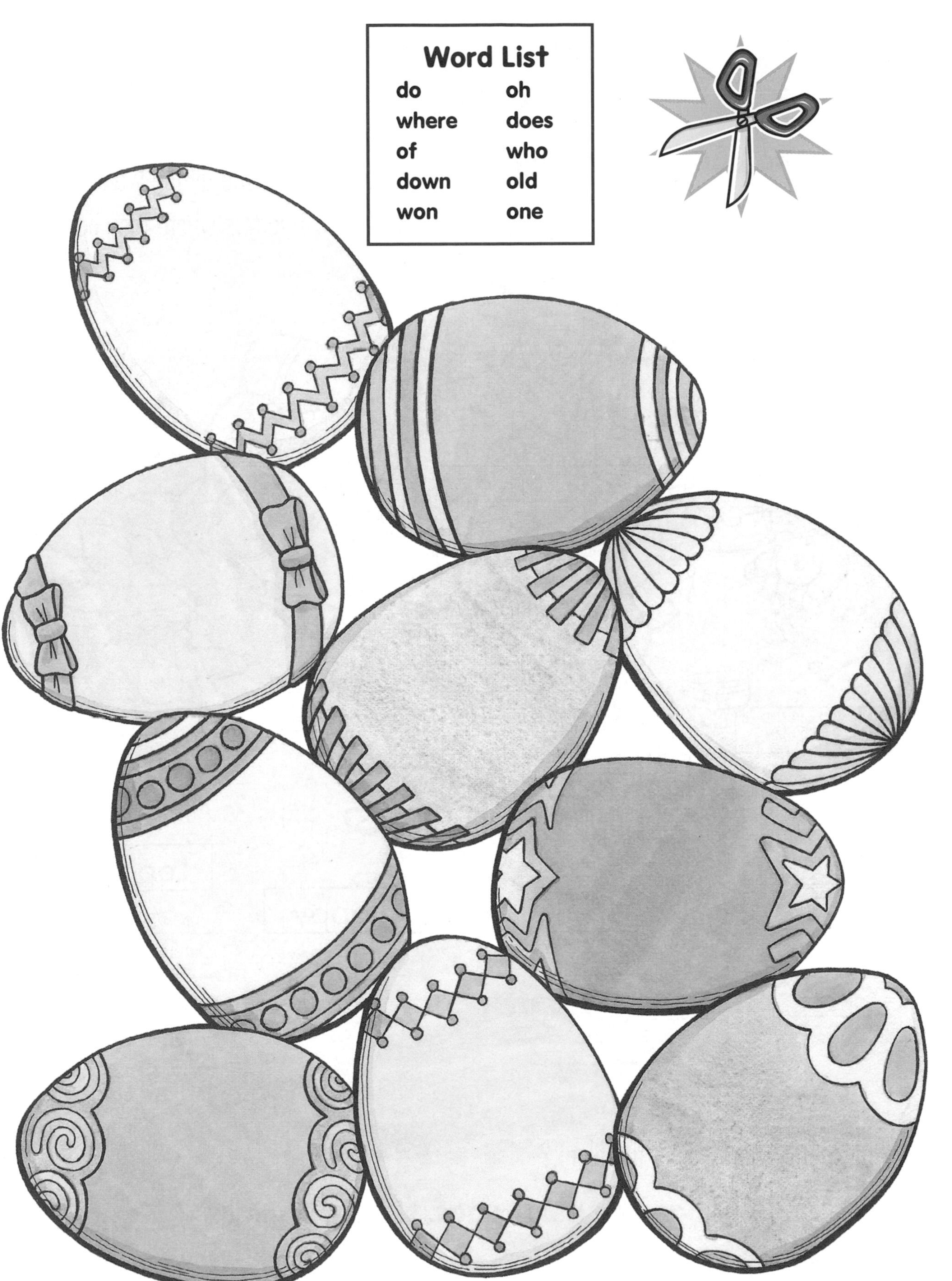

Egg Sort

Help the bunnies sort eggs.

Look at the number on each bunny. Look at the eggs. Sort the spelling words by counting the number of letters in the word on each egg. Write all the words with 2, 3, 4, and 5 letters where they belong.

What 3-letter word fills in the blank?

Hoppy Bunny has the most eggs. Hoppy Bunny ____________ the egg-sorting contest.

Ready for Rain

Look at the words on the raincoats and boots. Match the raincoat to the pair of boots with the same spelling word on them. Draw a line from the raincoat to the matching boots.

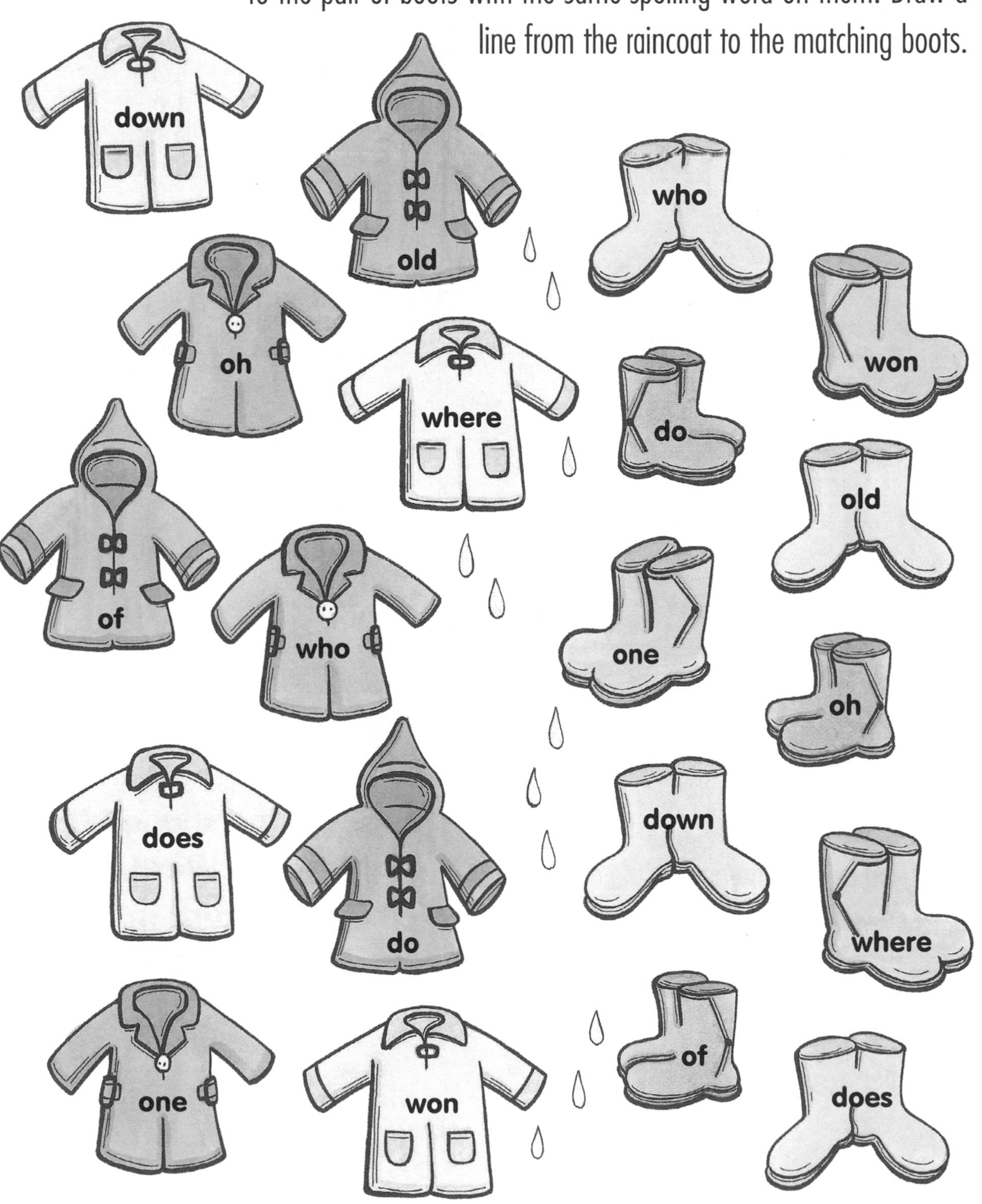

Puzzled

Use the Word List to fill in the puzzle.

Word List

do	oh
where	does
of	who
down	old
won	one

	1.				
		2.			
	3.				
4.					
	5.				

1. not up

2. what you ask when you don't know a person's name

3. She __________her best work.

4. what you ask when you don't know a place

5. a number

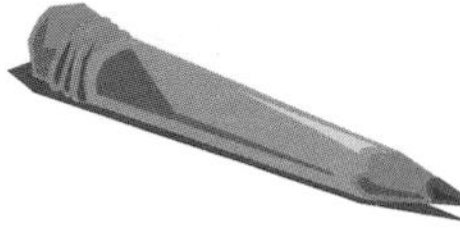

Look at the shaded letters. They spell a Word List word. Write the word in the blank.

__________________ did Easter Bunny hide my basket?

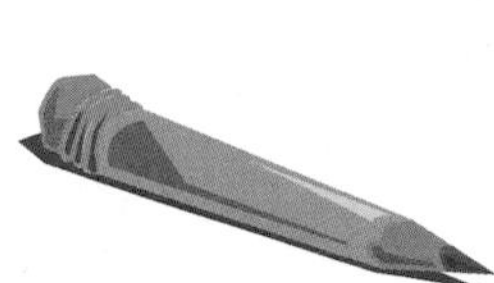

A Dandy Sort

Dandy Duck is sorting the Word List spelling words. Help Dandy put the Word List words where they belong. Note: four words are used more than once.

Words that begin with d

Words that begin with o

Words that begin with w

Words that end with o

Words that end with n

Baskets Full of Easter Joy

Help Easter Bunny fill the baskets. Trace the word. Then look for the word in old magazines, newspapers, and catalogs. Cut out the word and glue the word to the basket. Do your best to find as many as you can for each word.

Note: If you have trouble finding a word, you may write the word on paper, then cut the word out and glue it on the basket.

who

does

where

do

old

of

won

oh

down

one

Party Time

Think of the words in this practice set. Can you spell them? Show what you know!

A Birthday Party

One _____ (1.) my friends has a little brother. His brother will be ________ (2.) year ________ (3.). He is having a birthday party. My friend asked me to come to the party, but I don't know __________ (4.) he lives.

I hope my mom _____________ (5.). He said he lives __________ (6.) by the lake. There are only three houses there, so it can't be too hard to find. ________ (7.) boy! I hope we play fun games. At the last party I went to, I _________ (8.) a prize. _______ (9.) knows, maybe I will win again. I like to go to parties. __________ (10.) you like to go to parties, too?

The animals of the forest are having a party. Little rabbit is turning a year old. Turn the page to see if you spelled the words correctly.

Answers on the following page.

I hope you spelled every word correctly!

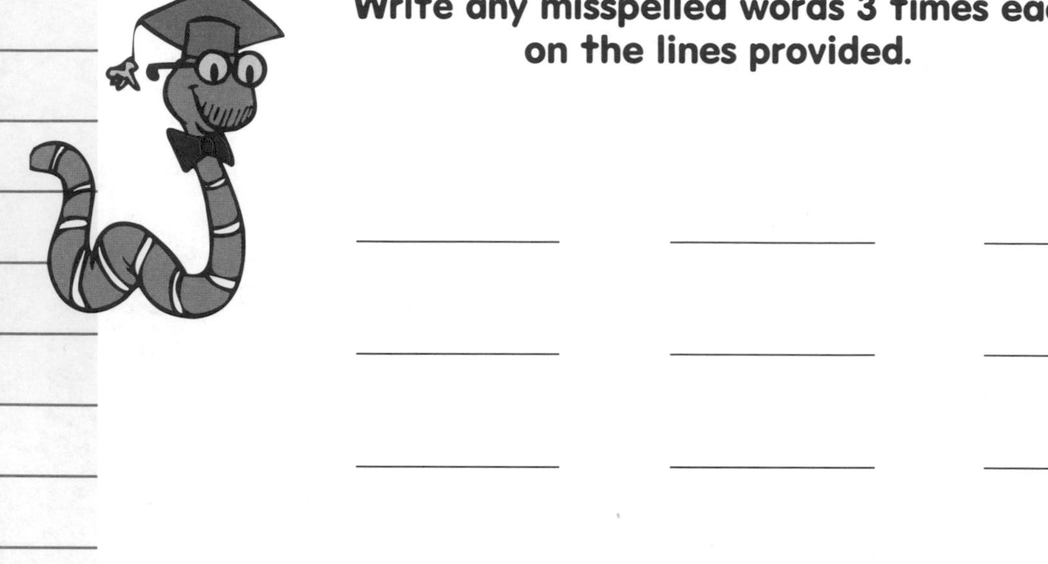

Write any misspelled words 3 times each on the lines provided.

Answers

1. of 2. one 3. old 4. where 5. does 6. down 7. Oh 8. won 9. Who 10. Do

The Very Wordy Caterpillars

Word List

lose	through
because	love
very	book
many	walk
both	money

Find the words hidden on the caterpillars. Write the words on the blanks.

loslovewbemanybiboth

verthoruthroughlooeloset

walbecausevorverythroufh

bokbookmamoneywowalk

Flower Power

Look at the words written with flowers. Write the word on the line next to it. Color the flowers that form each word.

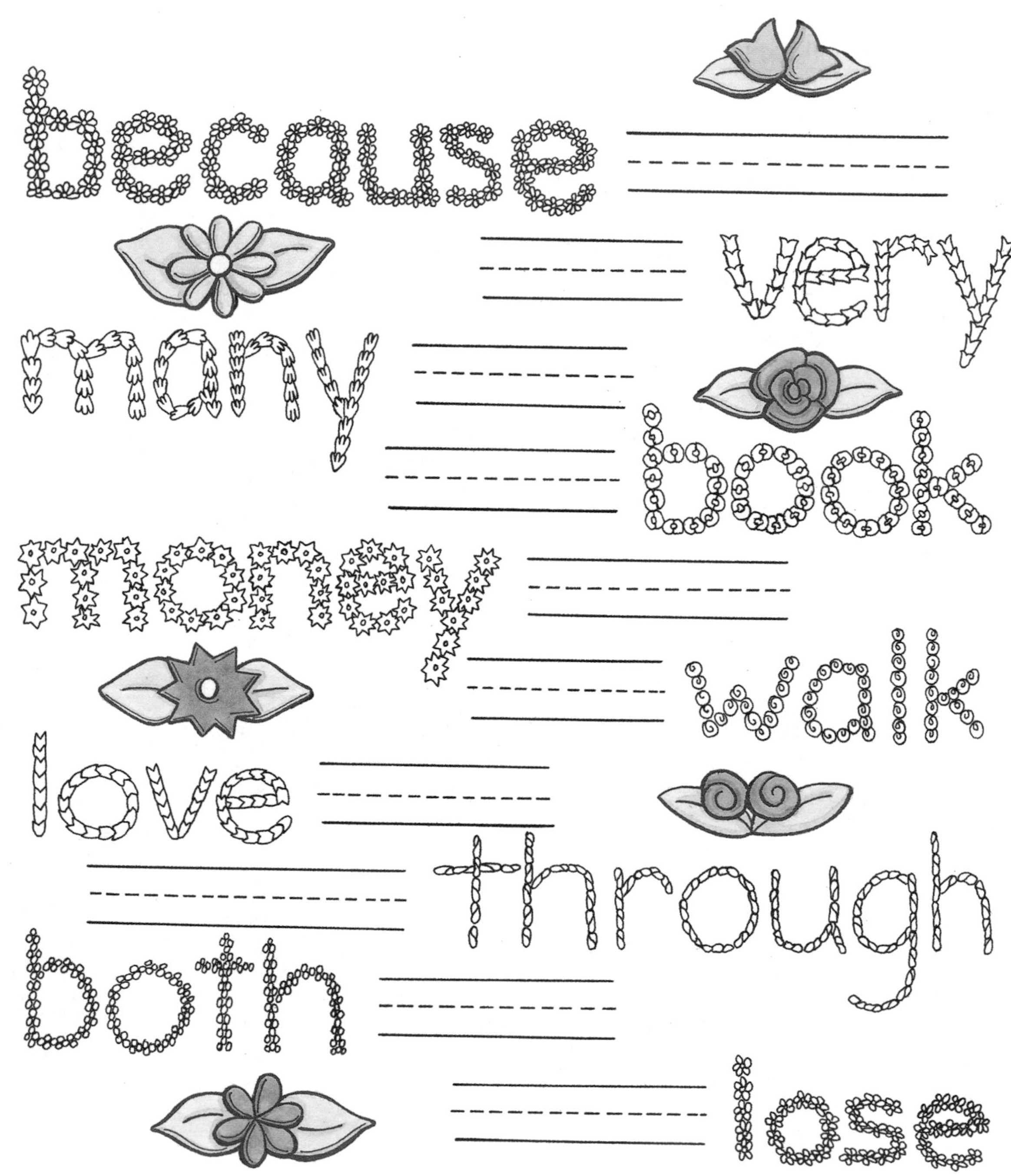

Spring into Math Spelling!

Math + Spelling = Fun

Look at the problems below. Add and subtract to find the spelling word. Write it on the line next to the problem. **Note:** One word is used twice.

look – ok + se = ________

money + a – oney + ny = ________

both – th + ok = ________

lose – se + ve = ________

love - lo + ry = ________

because – ecause + oth = ________

both – bo + rough = ________

walk – wak + ose = ________

Welcome to My Garden!

Write the words on the flower petals. Use your favorite writing tool.
Color the flowers when you are finished.

very
walk
many
because
both

All Abuzz

Look at the bees and the hives. Look at the words on each bee and each hive. Circle the hive that matches the word on the bee.

Where's My Lunch?

Help Bitty Ant find her way to the picnic. Follow the path with all the words spelled correctly. Use the Word List to help you.

Word List	
lose	**through**
because	**love**
very	**book**
many	**walk**
both	**money**

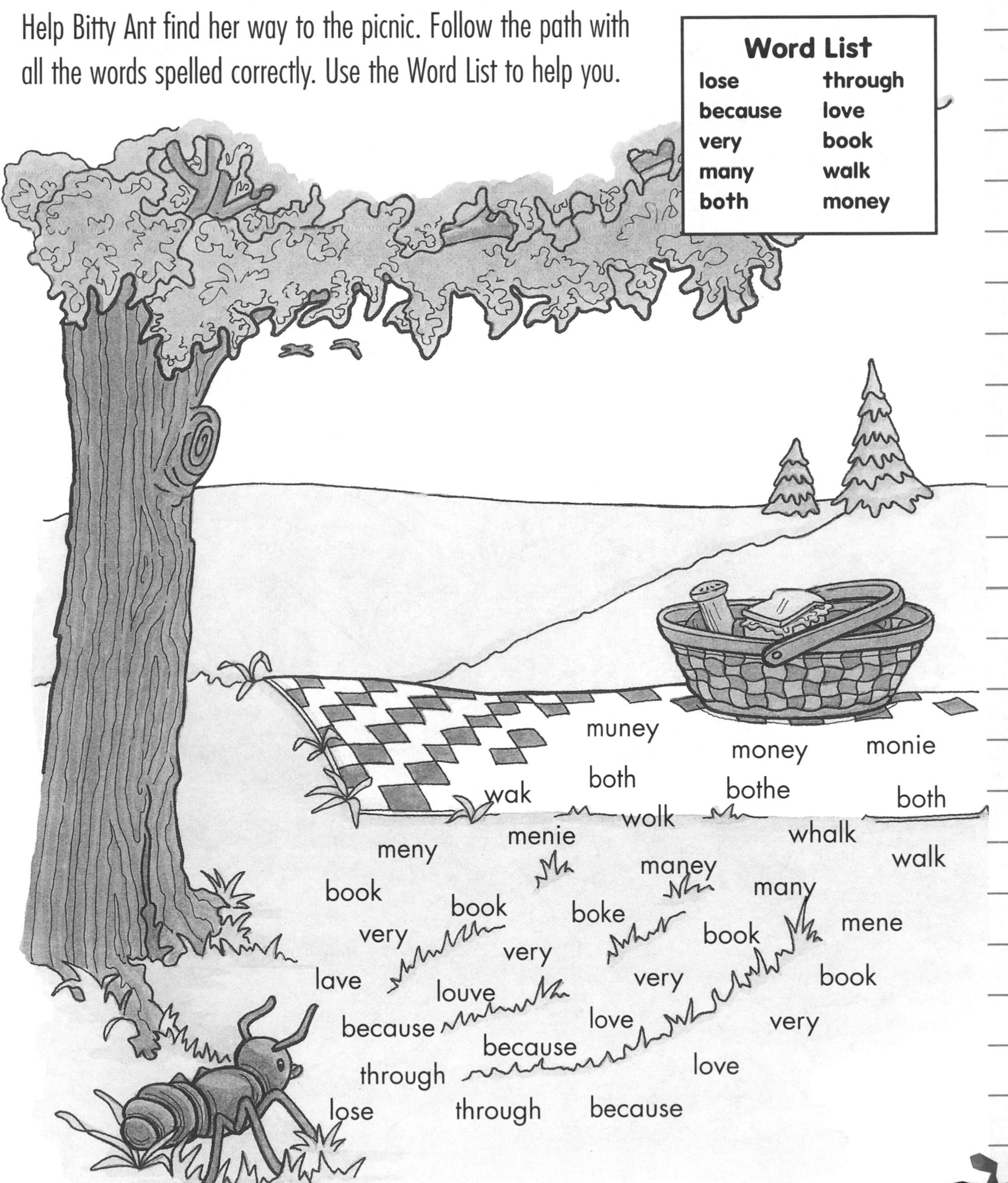

Here Comes the Sun!

Fill in the missing letters to form spelling words.

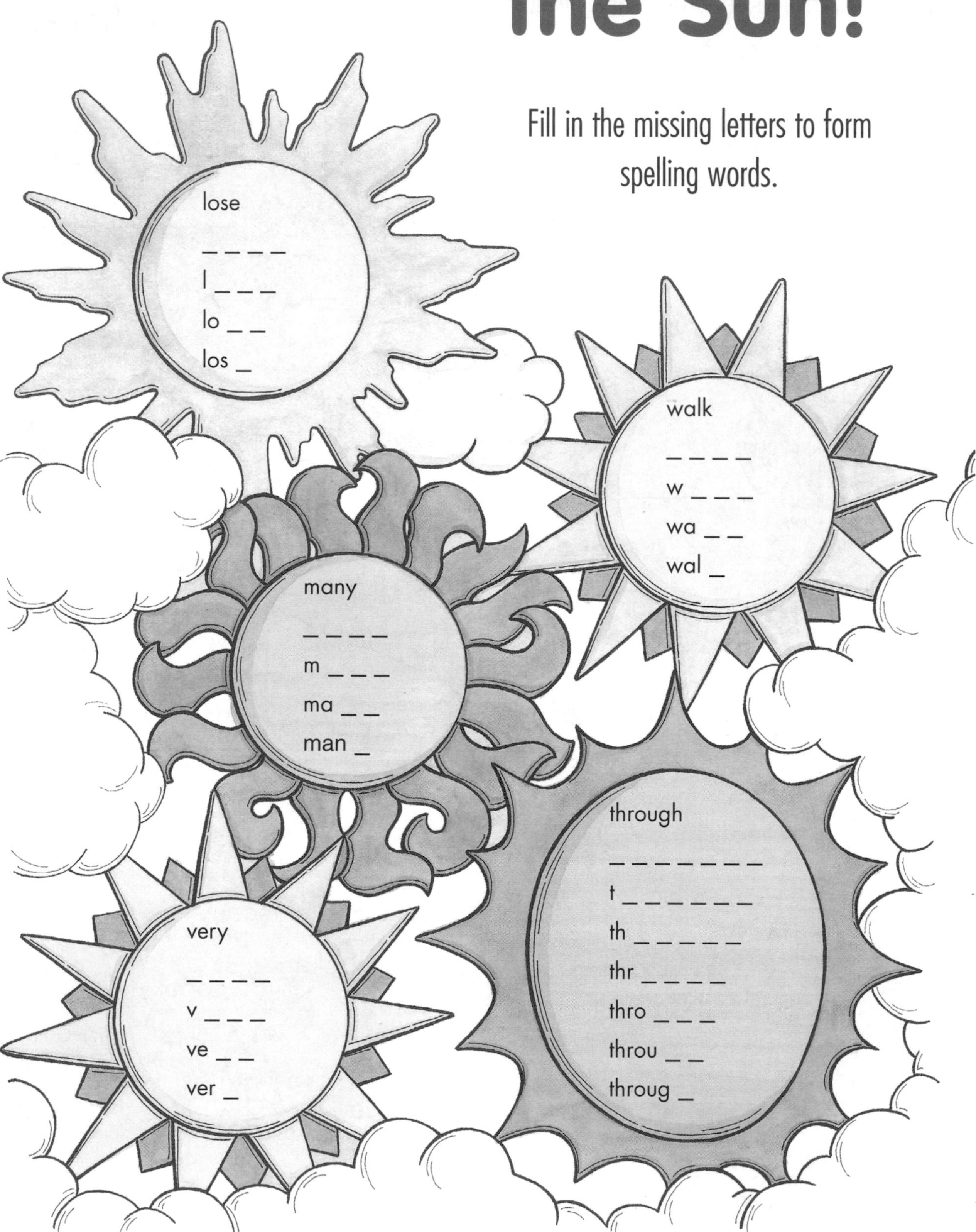

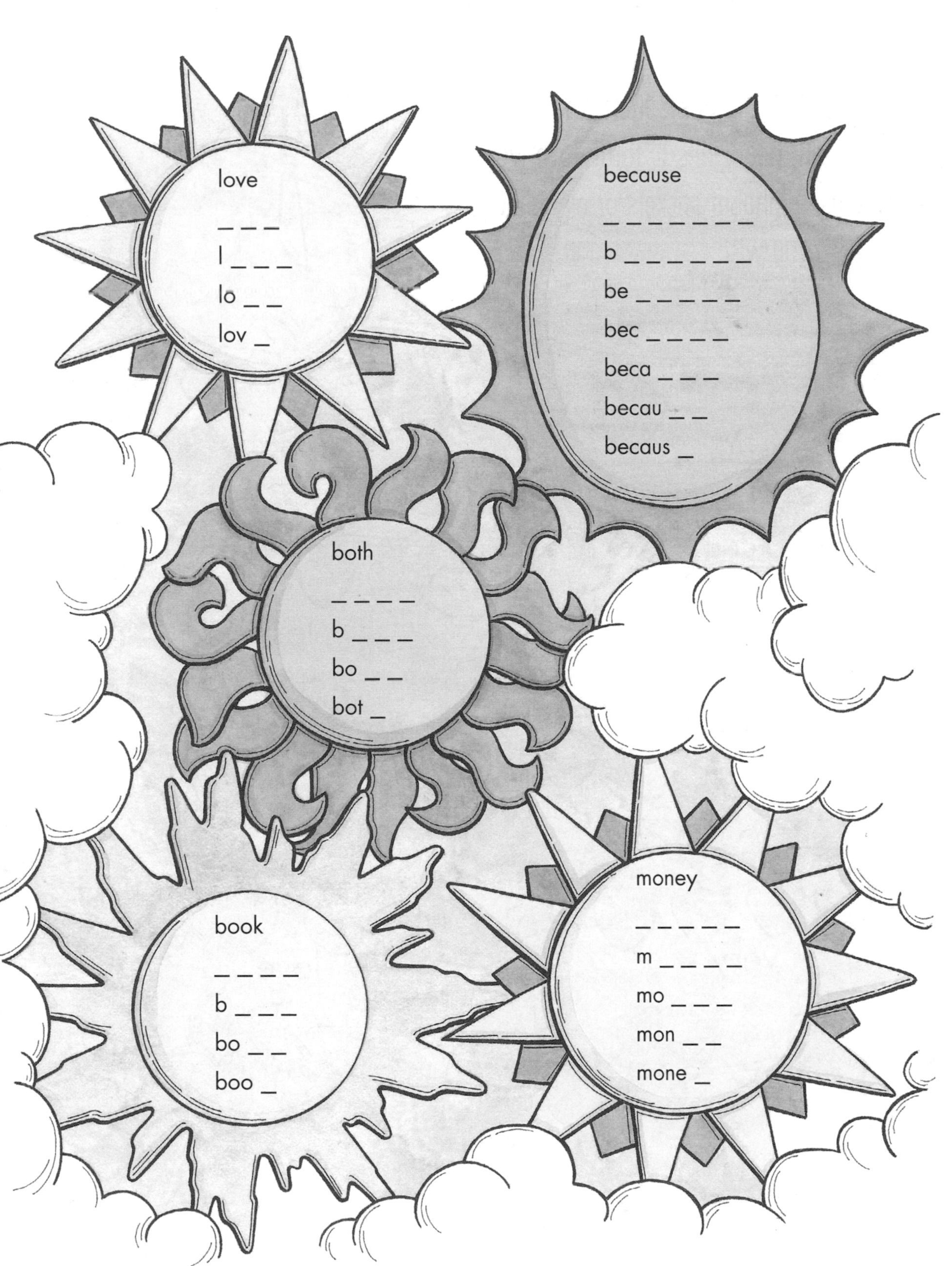
love
___
l ___
lo __
lov _
because
____
b ______
be _____
bec ____
beca ___
becau __
becaus _
both
____
b ___
bo __
bot _
book
____
b ___
bo __
boo _
money
_____
m ____
mo ___
mon __
mone _

Fresh on the Vine!

Build the word. Cut the letters from catalogs, newspapers, and magazines to form each word. Or you may use alphabet stickers or alphabet letter stamps if you wish.

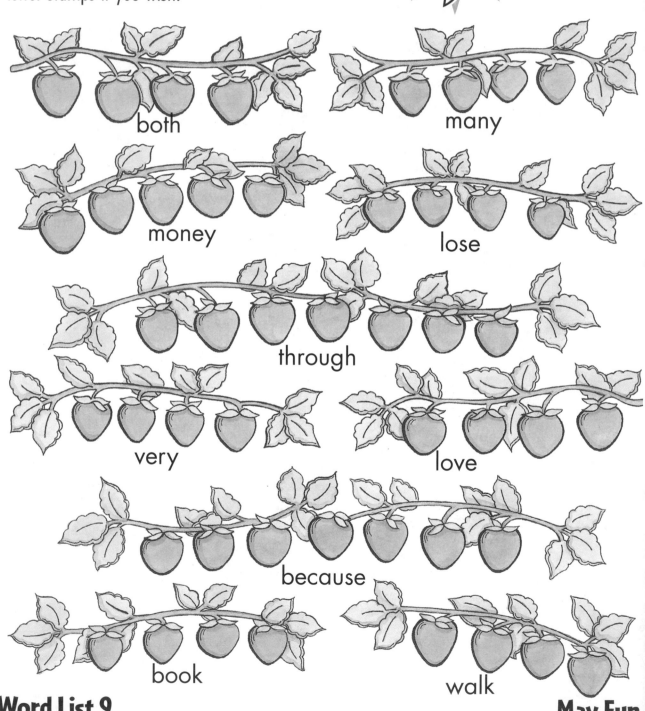

both

many

money

lose

through

very

love

because

book

walk

Spring Into Action

Can you spell your words? Think of Word List 9. Answer the riddles and fill in the blanks below. Use a word from Word List 9.

Riddles

1. to not win ____________________
2. A tunnel is something you go ____________________.
3. What spelling word rhymes with honey? ____________________

Fill in the blank.

1. I like spring, ____________ it is warm.
2. I ____________ to smell the flowers.
3. The flowers smell __________ sweet.
4. I like to read a ____________ in the fresh spring air.
5. I read __________ kinds of books.
6. After I read, I like to go for a ____________ in the park with my two best friends.
7. Here is a picture of _________ my friends and me at the park.

Answers on the following page.

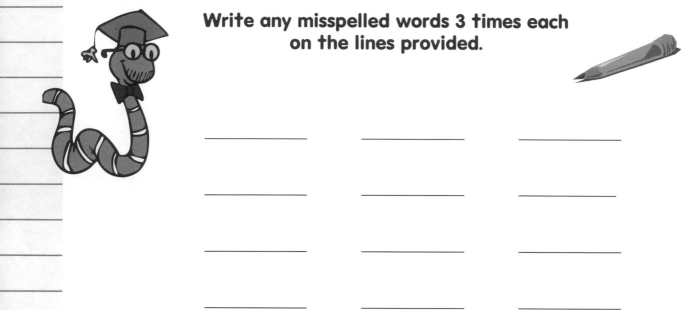

I hope you spelled every word correctly!

Write any misspelled words 3 times each on the lines provided.

____________	____________	____________
____________	____________	____________
____________	____________	____________
____________	____________	____________
____________	____________	____________
____________	____________	____________
____________	____________	____________
____________	____________	____________
____________	____________	____________
____________	____________	____________
____________	____________	____________

Answers

1. lose 2. through 3. money

1. because 2. love 3. very 4. book 5. many 6. walk 7. both

Fun-in-the-Sun Codes

Use the code to write the spelling words.

1. 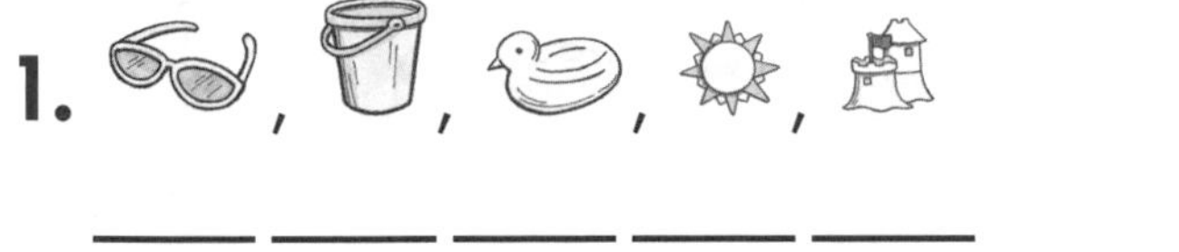

   ____ ____ ____ ____ ____

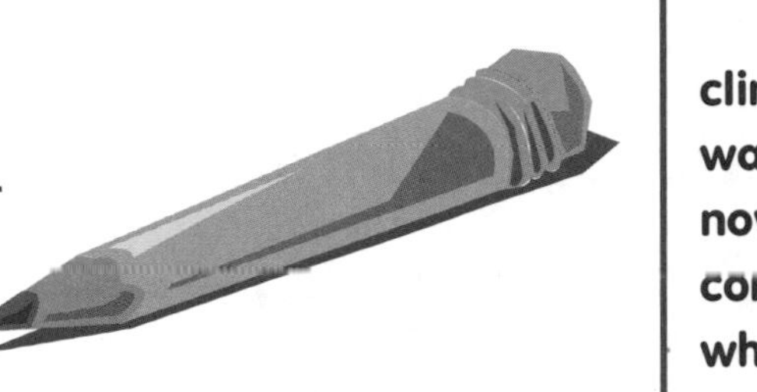

Word List	
climb	new
water	color
now	were
come	some
what	could

2. ____ ____ ____ ____

3. ____ ____ ____

4. 

   ____ ____ ____ ____

5. 

   ____ ____ ____ ____

6. 

   ____ ____ ____ ____

7. 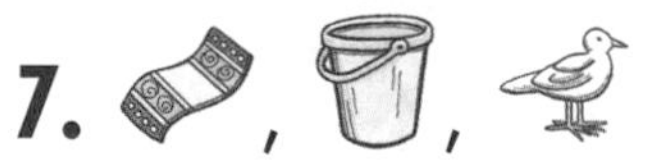

   ____ ____ ____

8. 

   ____ ____ ____ ____ ____

9. 

   ____ ____ ____ ____ ____

10. 

    ____ ____ ____ ____ ____

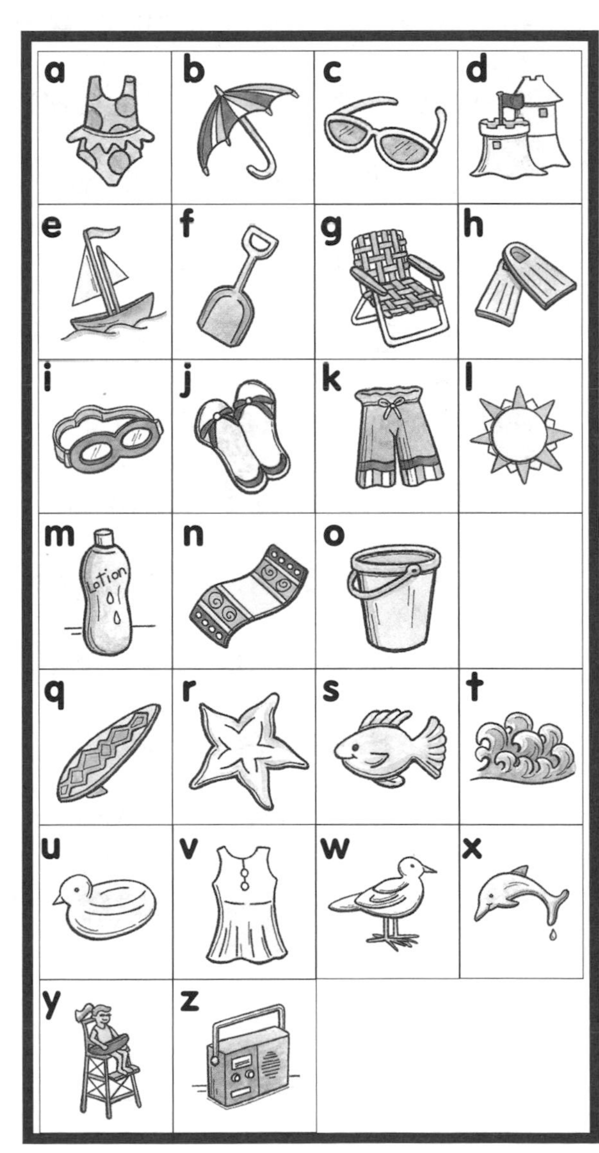

Beach Blanket Spello

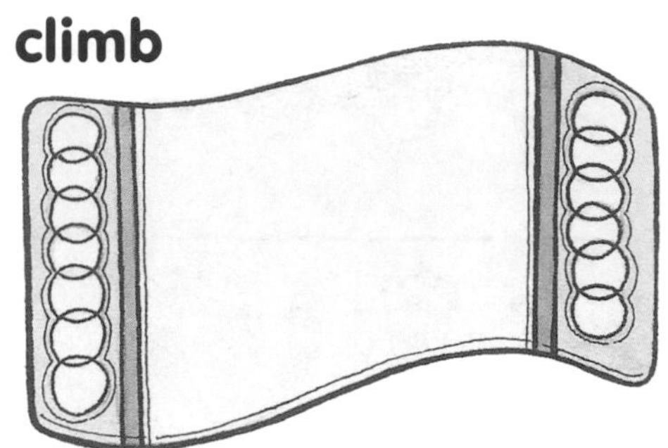

Be a beach super sleuth! Search for the word written next to each blanket. Use catalogs, newspapers, and magazines. Cut and then paste the word on the blanket or build the word letter by letter if you wish. Another fun idea is to write the word using a fancy paint or glitter pen, or to write the word with glue and sprinkle glitter on it. Be creative! Make each blanket a masterpiece.

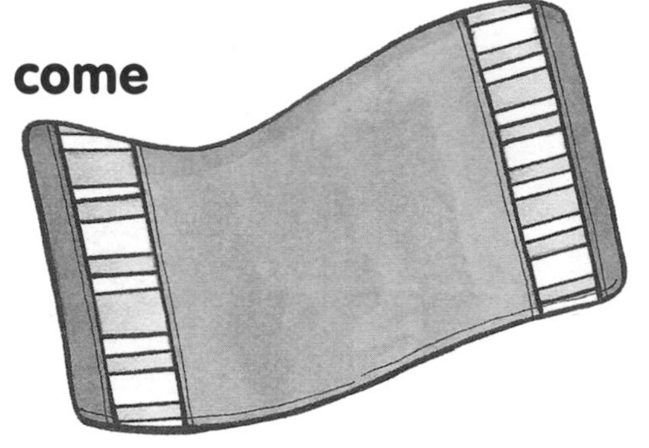

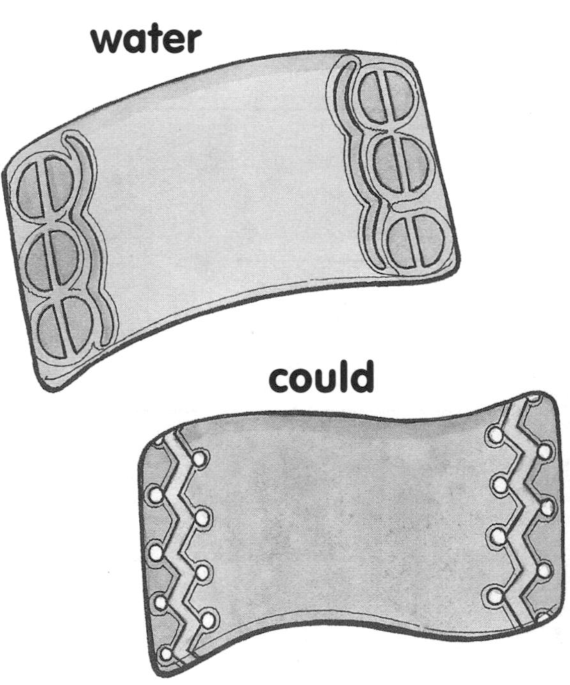

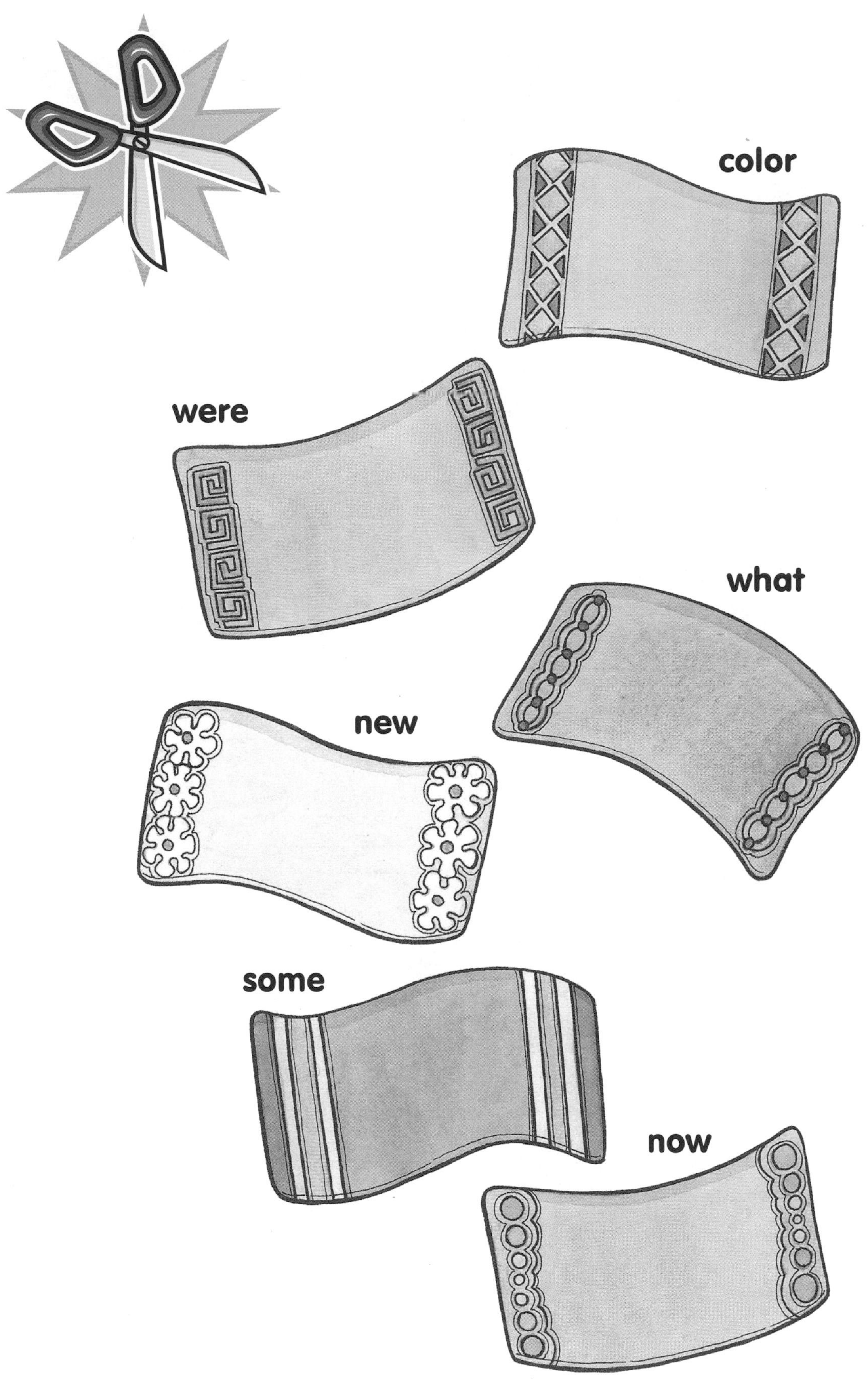
color
were
what
new
some
now

Dig into Spelling!

Write the spelling word around the shovels and pails.

Have a Ball!

Trace the spelling word. Then write the word three times. Use your favorite writing tools. Color the beach balls for added fun.

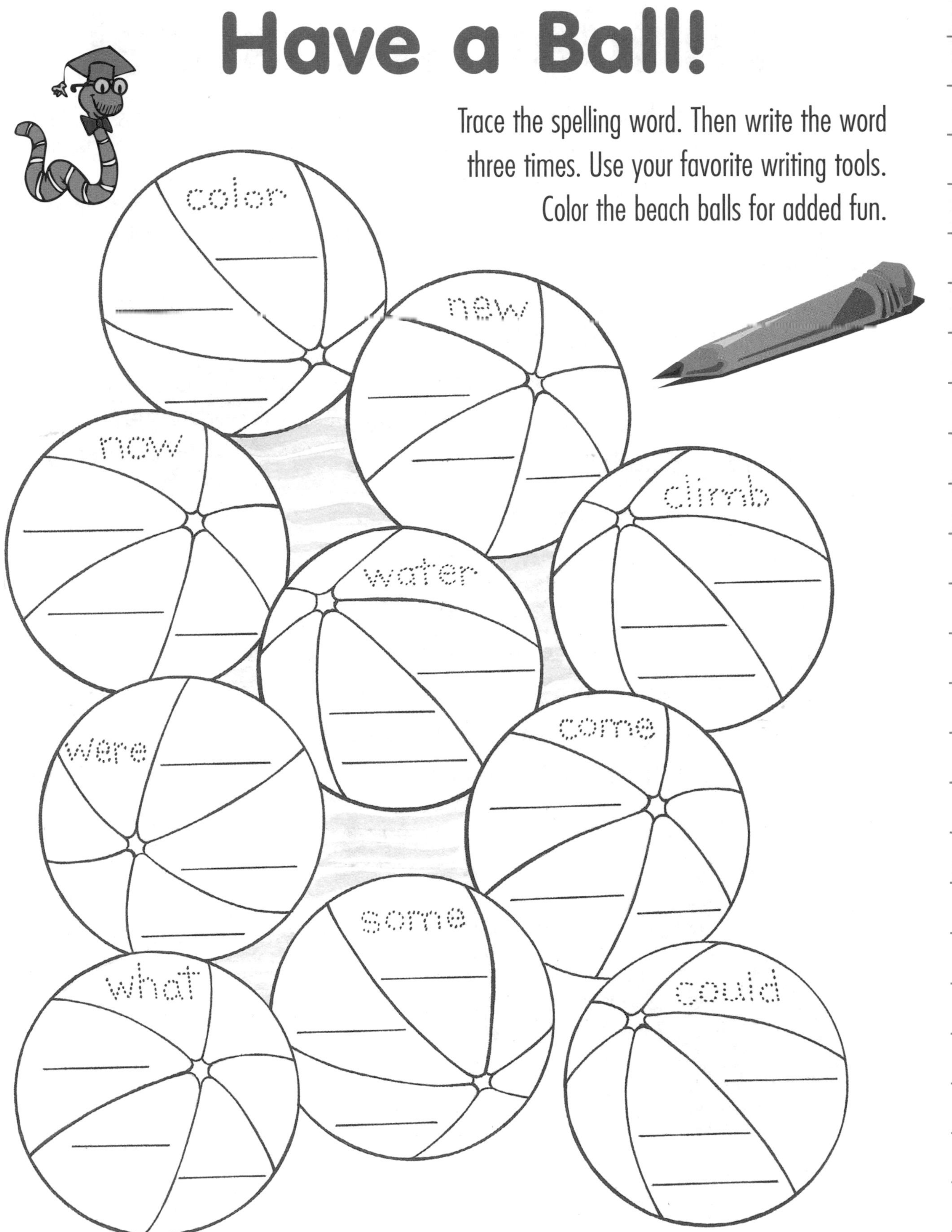

Hidden Treasure!

Many creatures live on the beach in the sand and in the water. They blend in so well, it is hard to tell they are there. Your spelling words are trying to blend in with the other words. Be a word detective! Find all the spelling words hidden in the story and its title.

Circle each spelling word. Use Word List 10 to help you. Write the words on the blanks below.

Where Could It Be?

The water at the beach feels great! The sun does, too. Grab your suit and a towel, and come and have some fun!

The sea is the perfect color of blue. It is so clear, you never can tell what you might see.

Climb aboard a boat. It doesn't matter if it's old or new. Go for a ride out on the waves as if you were a pirate. Look out over the sea with your spyglass to your eye. Now, just where was it that you hid your silver and your gold?

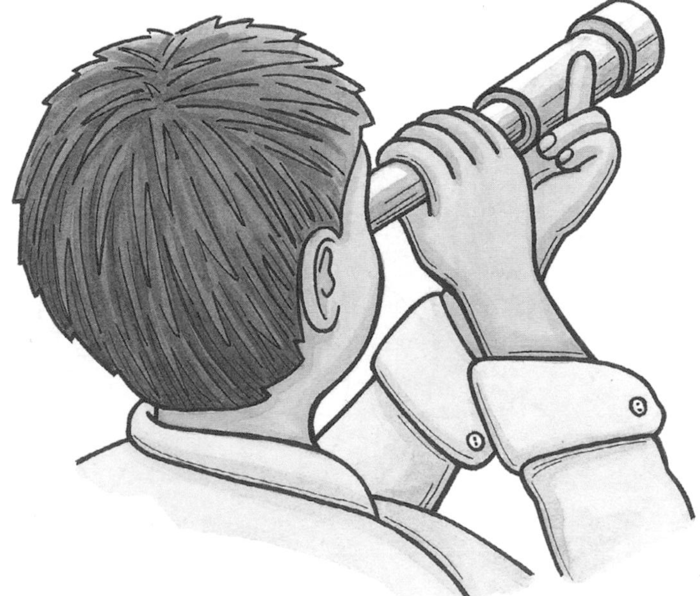

Toasty Word Shapes

Camping out is fun.
Campfires help campers cook and keep warm.

Word List	
climb	new
water	color
now	were
come	some
what	could

Look at the Word List words.
Look at the shape of each word. Fill in the boxes to form a spelling word that has the shape you see on the campfires.

Set Up Camp!

Which word on the tent does not match? Circle the word.

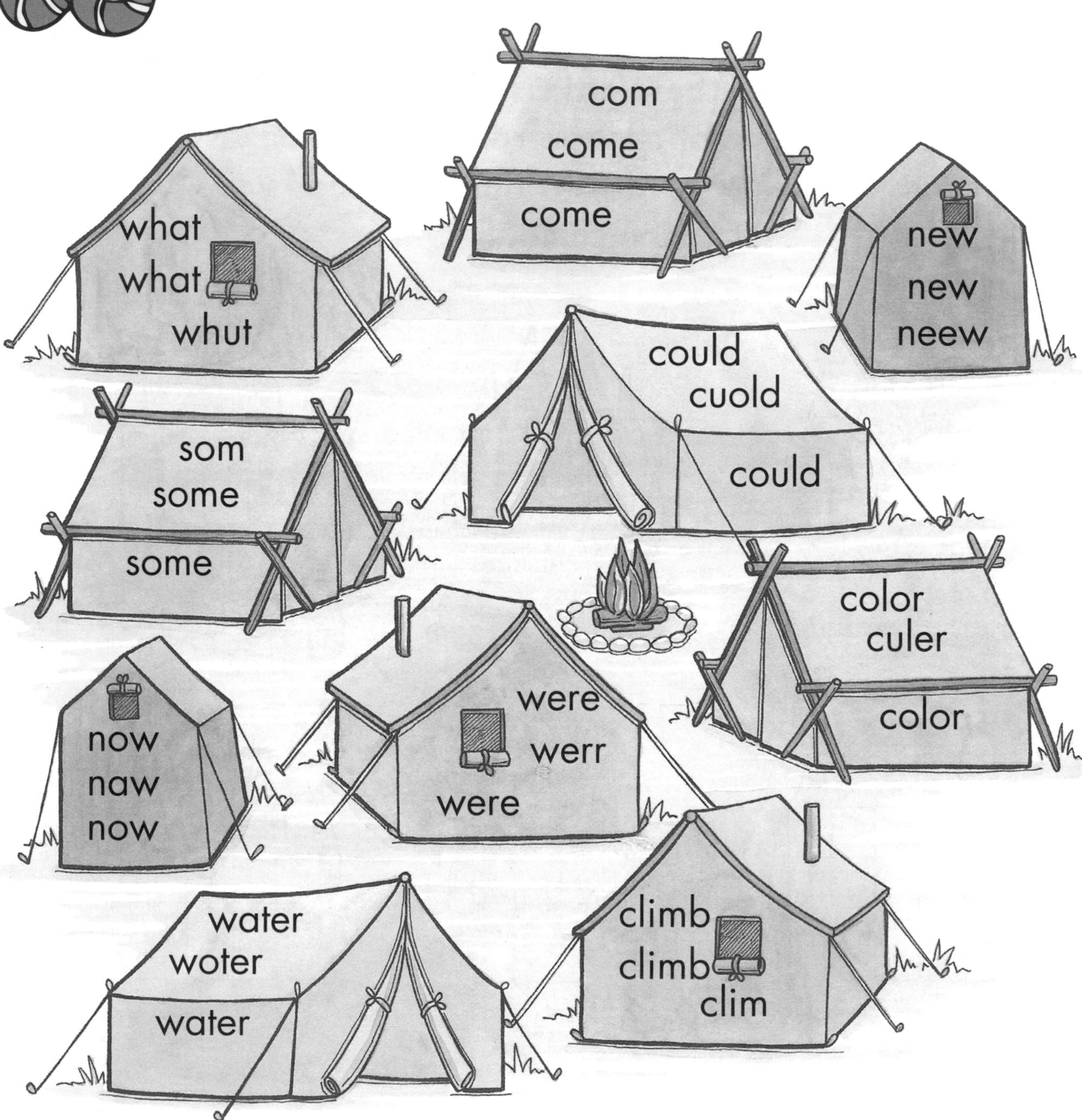

A Glow in the Dark!

Look at the fireflies.
If the word on the firefly is
spelled correctly,
color the tail section yellow.

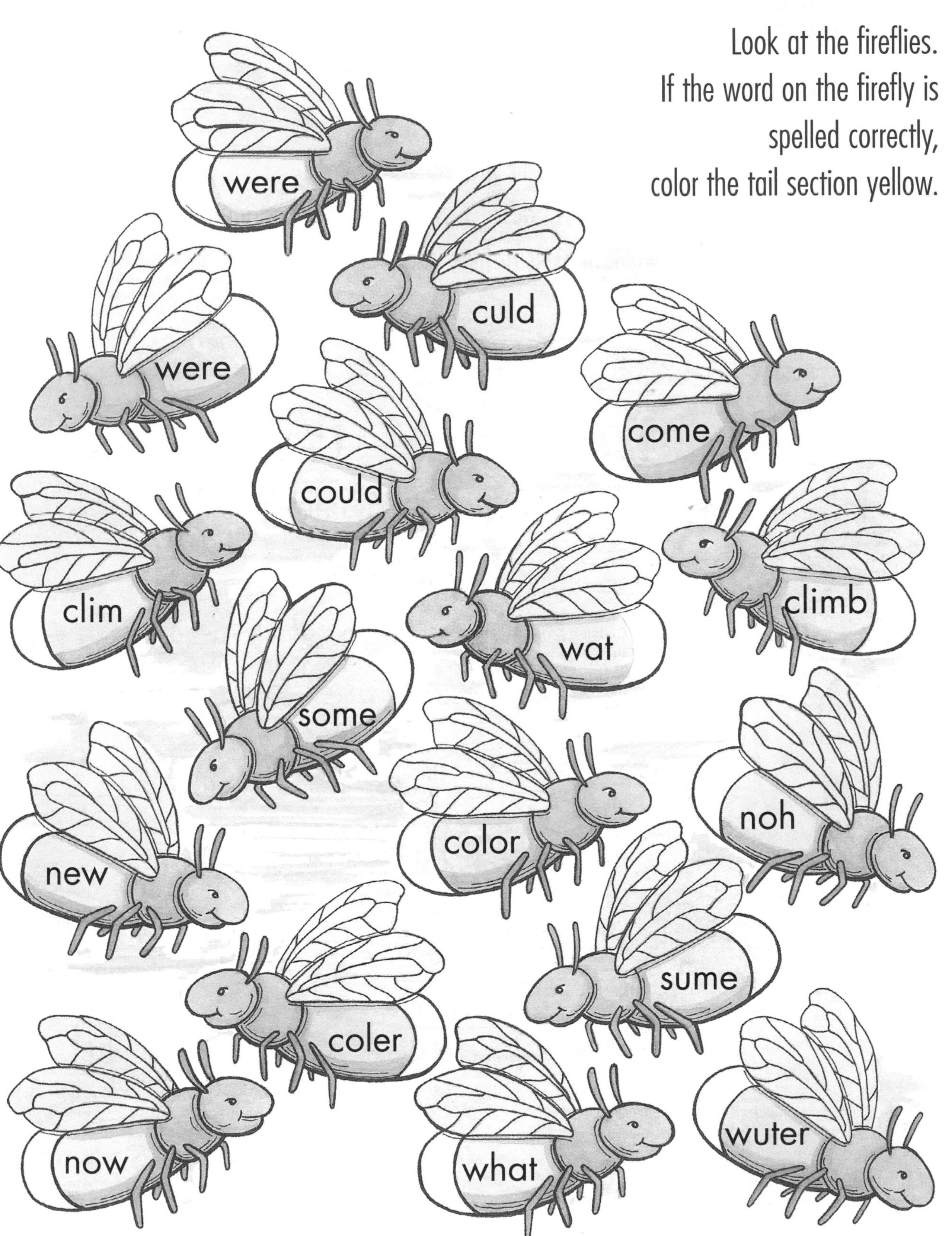

Don't Tip Your Canoe!

Stay afloat. Find the spelling words hidden on the canoes.
Use your Word List to help you.

Word List	
climb	new
water	color
now	were
come	some
what	could

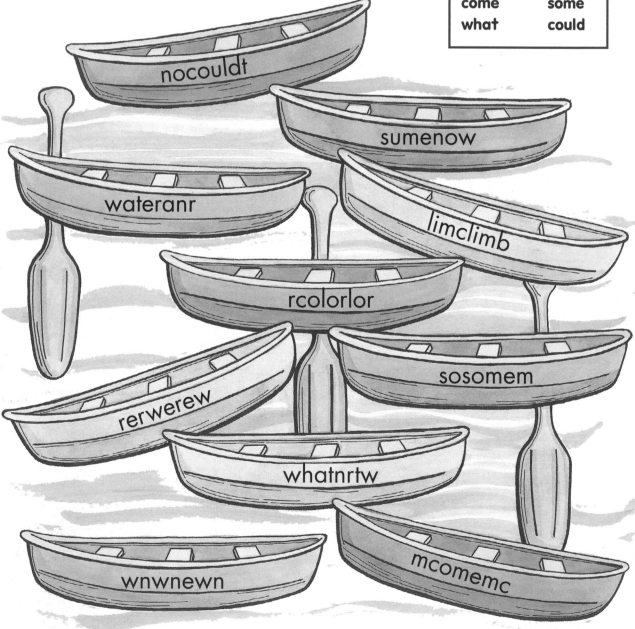

nocouldt

sumenow

wateranr

limclimb

rcolorlor

sosomem

rerwerew

whatnrtw

wnwnewn

mcomemc

Time to Show What You Know!

Think of Word List 10. Fill in the missing letters to form a word that fills in the blank. Use a word from Word List 10. Do your best to spell each word correctly. When you are finished, go to the following page to see if you filled in the missing letters correctly.

Camp Out

In the summer my family likes to go camping. We go hiking, too. We cl_ _ _ (1.) up many hills. We drink cold w _ _ _ _ (2.) from the stream on the trail.

We like to watch for animals in the forest. We are happy when we see s_ _ e (3.). You never can tell w_ _ t (4.) kind of animals you will see.

This year we will use our n_ _ (5.) tent. It c_ _ld (6.) hold an army! I love to camp out. It's neat to see wildflowers of every c_ _ _r (7.). I love to hear the gurgle of the stream.

When we c _m _ (8.) home, we think of our camping trip every n _ _ (9.) and then. Then we all say, "Oh, boy, we w_ r _ (10.) the best campers ever!"

I hope you spelled every word correctly!

Write any misspelled words 3 times each on the lines provided.

Answers

1. climb 2. water 3. some 4. what 5. new 6. could
7. color 8. come 9. now 10. were

Word List 1

September Fun Answer Key

Page 1. **It's Picking Time**

Word List 1

September Fun Answer Key

Page 2.

Football Puzzles

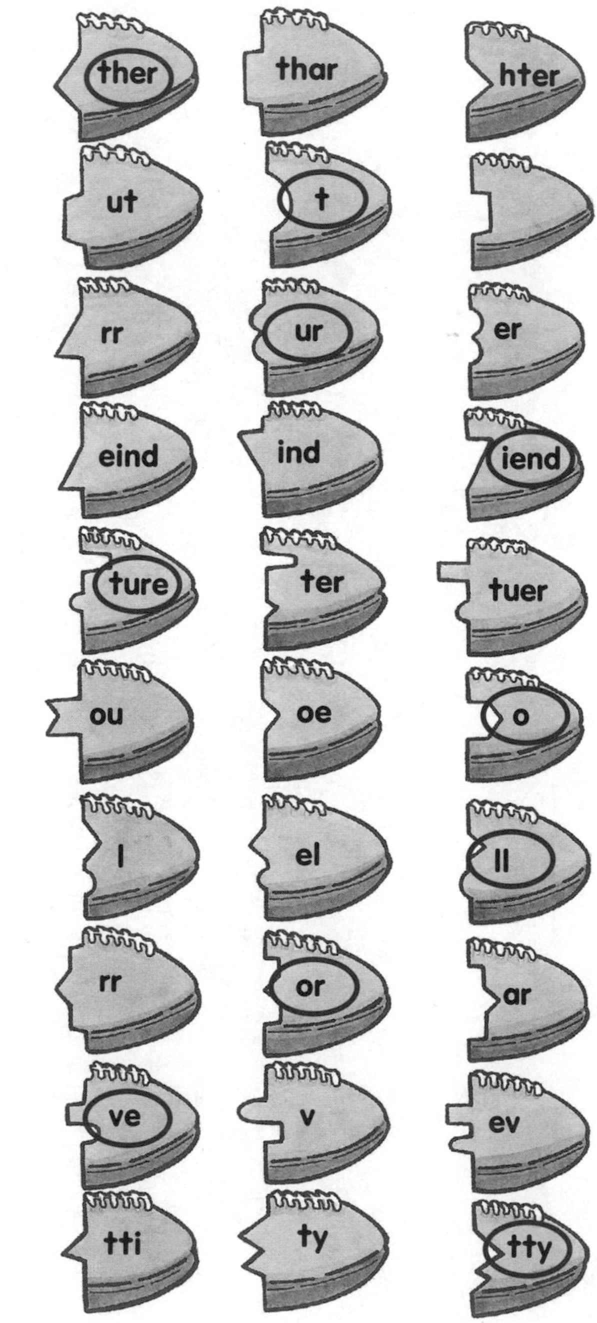

Word List 1

September Fun Answer Key

Page 3.

School Daze

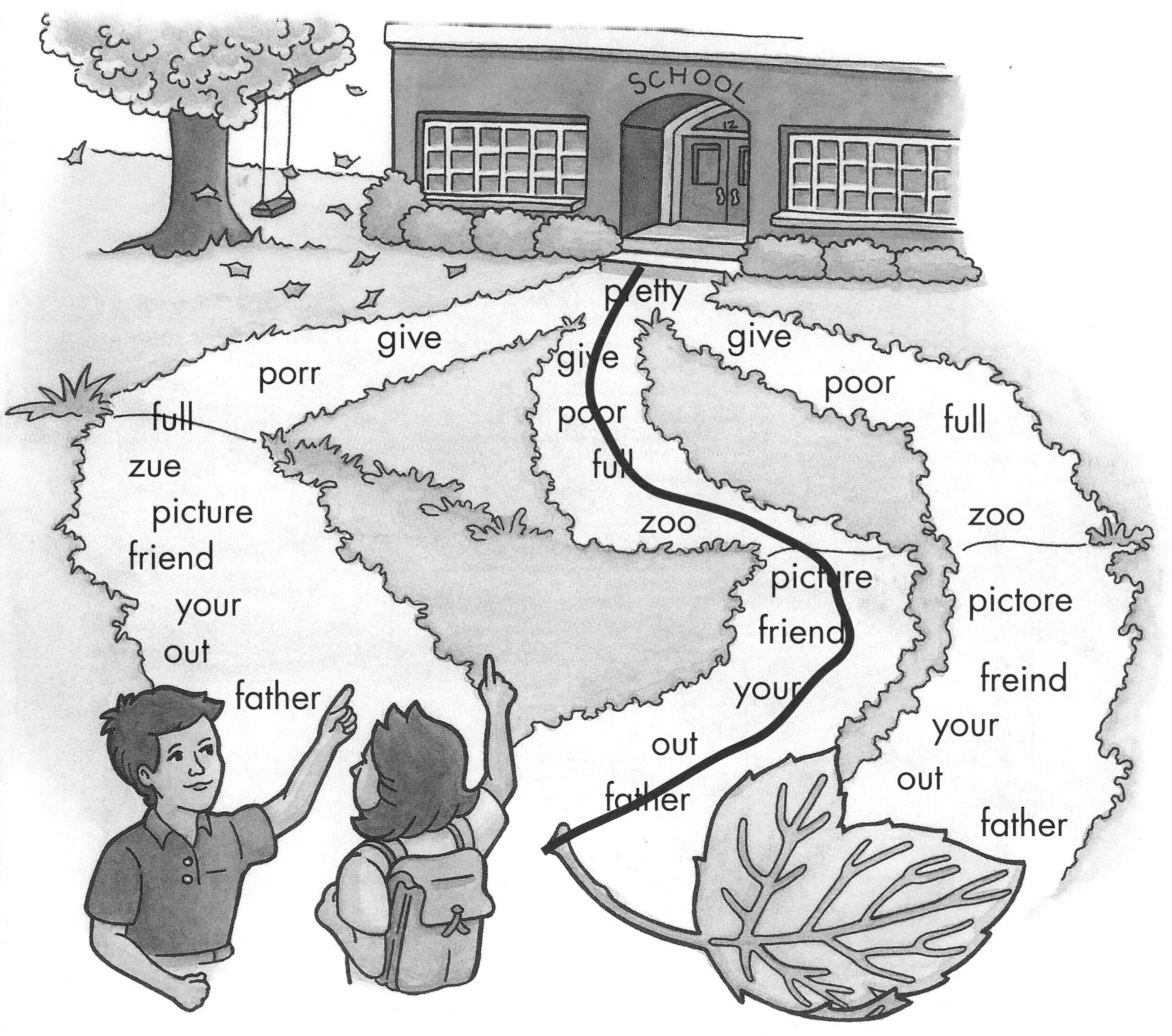

Word List 1

September Fun Answer Key

Page 4. **Supply the Correct Word**

1. picture 2. friend 3. out 4. give 5. father

6. pretty 7. zoo 8. full 9. poor 10. your

Page 5. **Lend a Hand**

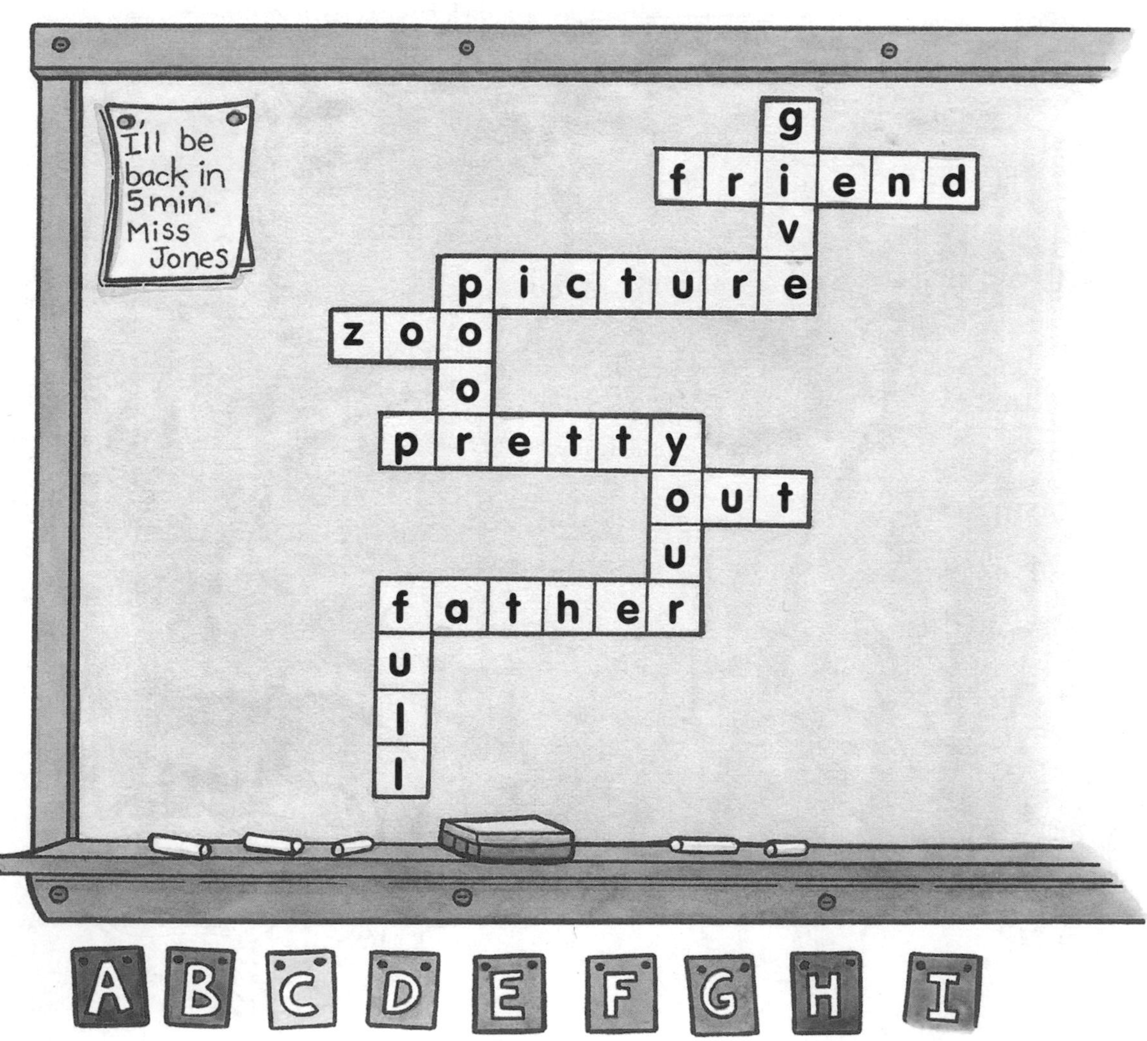

Word List 1

September Fun Answer Key

Page 6.

A Friendly Letter

Dear Joe,

I had a fun summer. I went to the [1] with my [2]. We got to see a lot of animals. I liked the deer the best. I took a [3] of them. They looked so [4]. The little ones had spots.

It was a hot day. The sun was out big and bright. The [5], hairy, ape looked so hot. I wanted to [6] him a fan.

After we left the zoo we ate at a diner. The diner had the best burgers and fries. Dad and I ate until we were too [7] to eat one more bite. It was a fun day!

[8] [9],

Todd

1. zoo
2. father
3. picture
4. pretty
5. poor
6. give
7. full
8. Your
9. friend

Word List 1

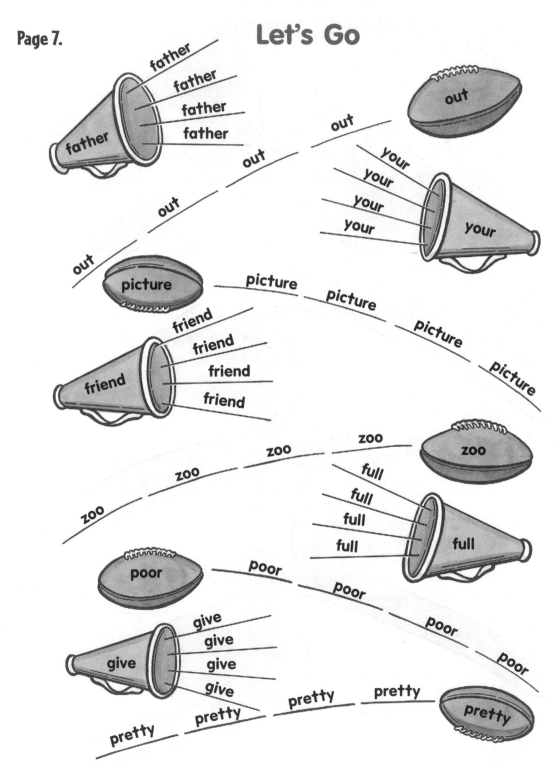

September Fun Answer Key

Page 7.

Let's Go

father father father father father

out out out out out out

your your your your your

picture picture picture picture picture

friend friend friend friend friend

zoo zoo zoo zoo zoo

full full full full full

poor poor poor poor poor

give give give give give

pretty pretty pretty pretty pretty

Word List 1

September Fun Answer Key

Page 8.

Chalk It Up!

Word List 1

September Fun Answer Key

Page 9.

Fall Help

"My father likes fall," said Tim. "He says the leaves are pritty."

"My fother does not like fall," said Ann. "He does not like to rake. It makes him tired, and then we have no time for fun."

"I giv him a hand, but por father still is beat," said Ann.

"Your yard is foll of trees. That makes it hard to keep it raked," said Tim. "You are my frend, Ann. I like to rake. Next time I will help your father rake."

"Good!" said Ann. "Then we will have more time to go to the zoe. Father and I love to go to the zoo. You can come with us."

"That is a deal," said Tim. "I will help the next time I see him otu raking."

"Father loves to take pictures at the zoo. He takes a pictuer of all the neat animals. I bet he will take yor picture, too."

"That is fine with me," said Tim. "I can't wait to go. I think I'll grab the rake and get going. He may want to go today!"

"I will give you a hand," said Ann with a smile. "I'm glad you are my friend. I bet my father will be glad I have a friend like you, too!"

Word List 1

September Fun Answer Key

Page 10.

Test Time!

1. A zoo is a place to see animals.
2. A father is a dad.
3. Out means not in.
4. A picture is a photo.
5. Your means belonging to you.
6. Poor means not rich.
7. Pretty means not ugly.
8. Friend means a pal.
9. Full means not empty.
10. Give means to hand to.

Word List 2

October Fun
Answer Key

Page 11.

Fall Yard Work

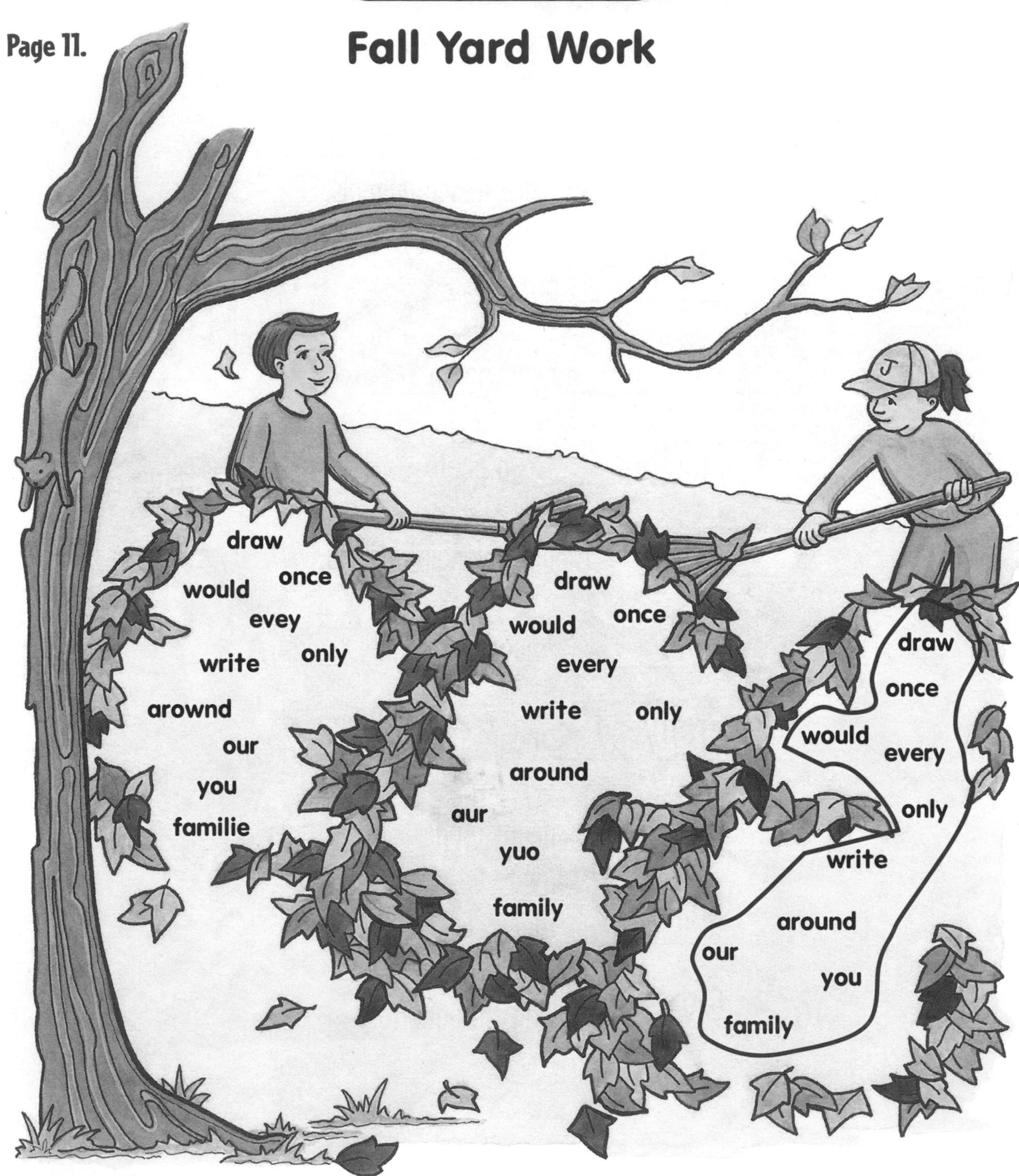

Word List 2

October Fun
Answer Key

Page 12.

Fall Code Crackers

= a, = c, = d, = e, = f, = g, = i,

= l, = m, = n, = o, = r, = t, = u,

= v, = w, = y

1. a r o u n d
2. y o u

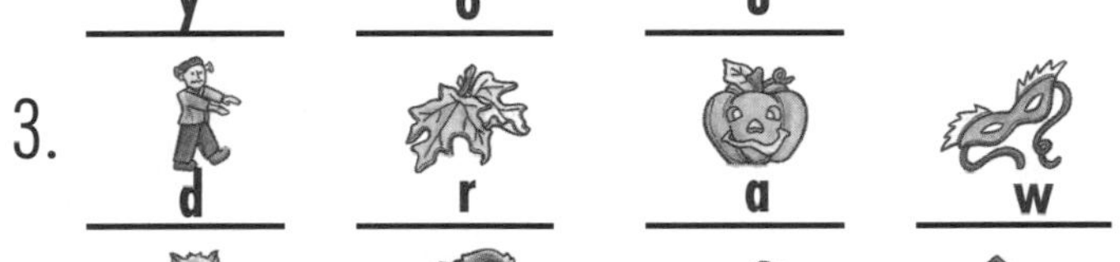

3. d r a w

4. o n l y
5. o n c e

6. f a m i l y
7. o u r

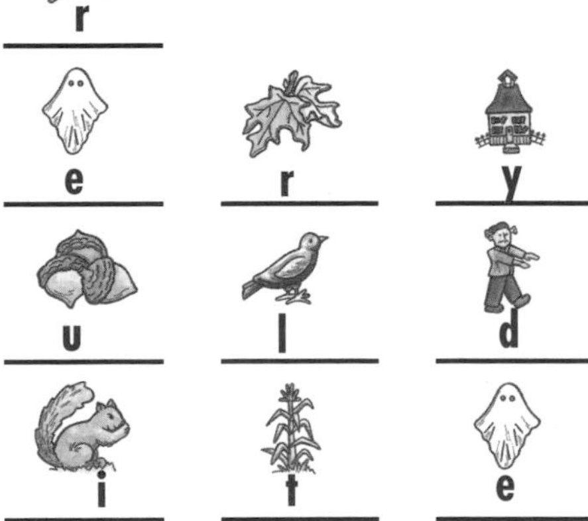

8. e v e r y
9. w o u l d
10. w r i t e

Word List 2

October Fun Answer Key

Page 13.

As The Crow Flies

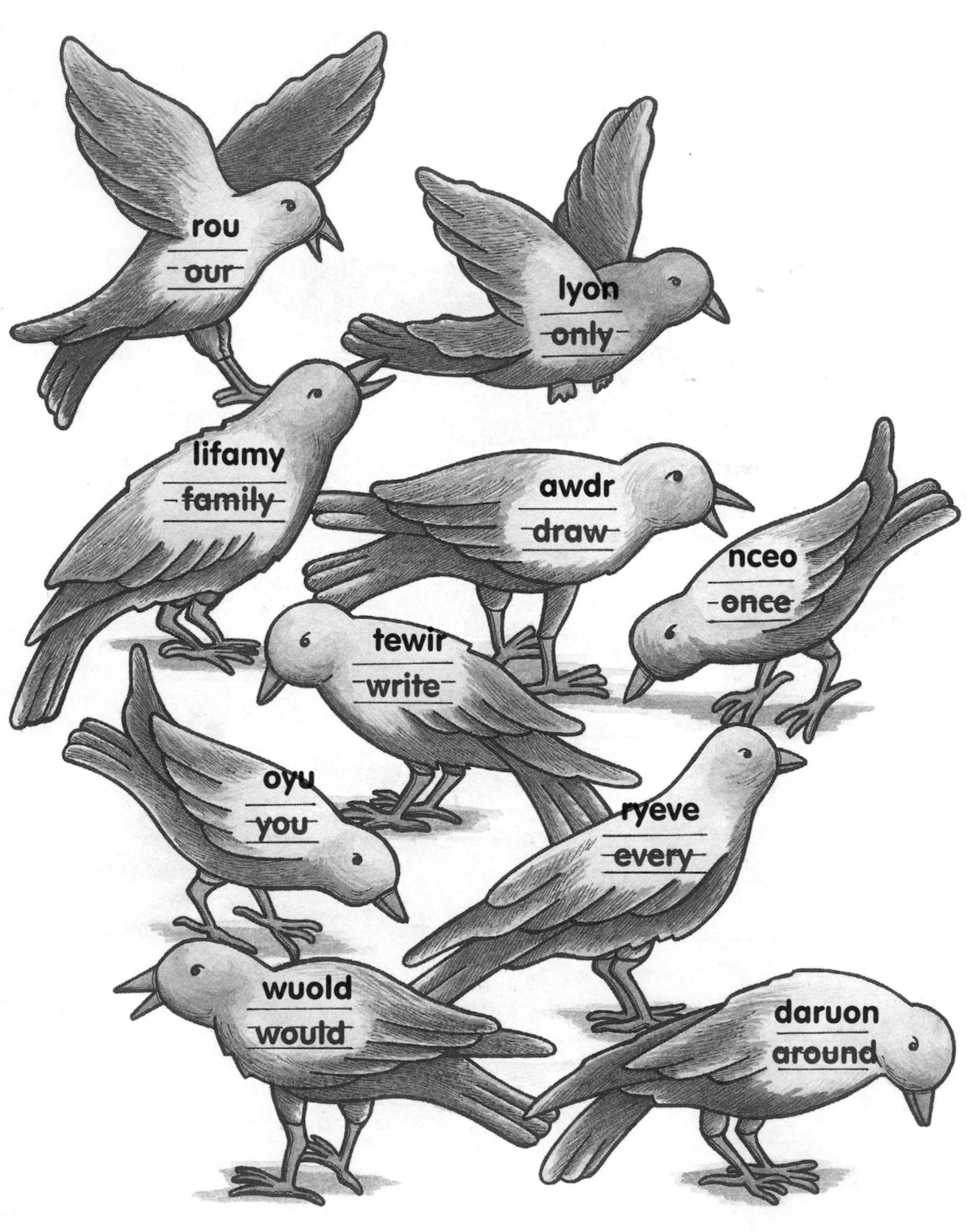

Word List 2

October Fun
Answer Key

Page 14.

Nuts About Spelling

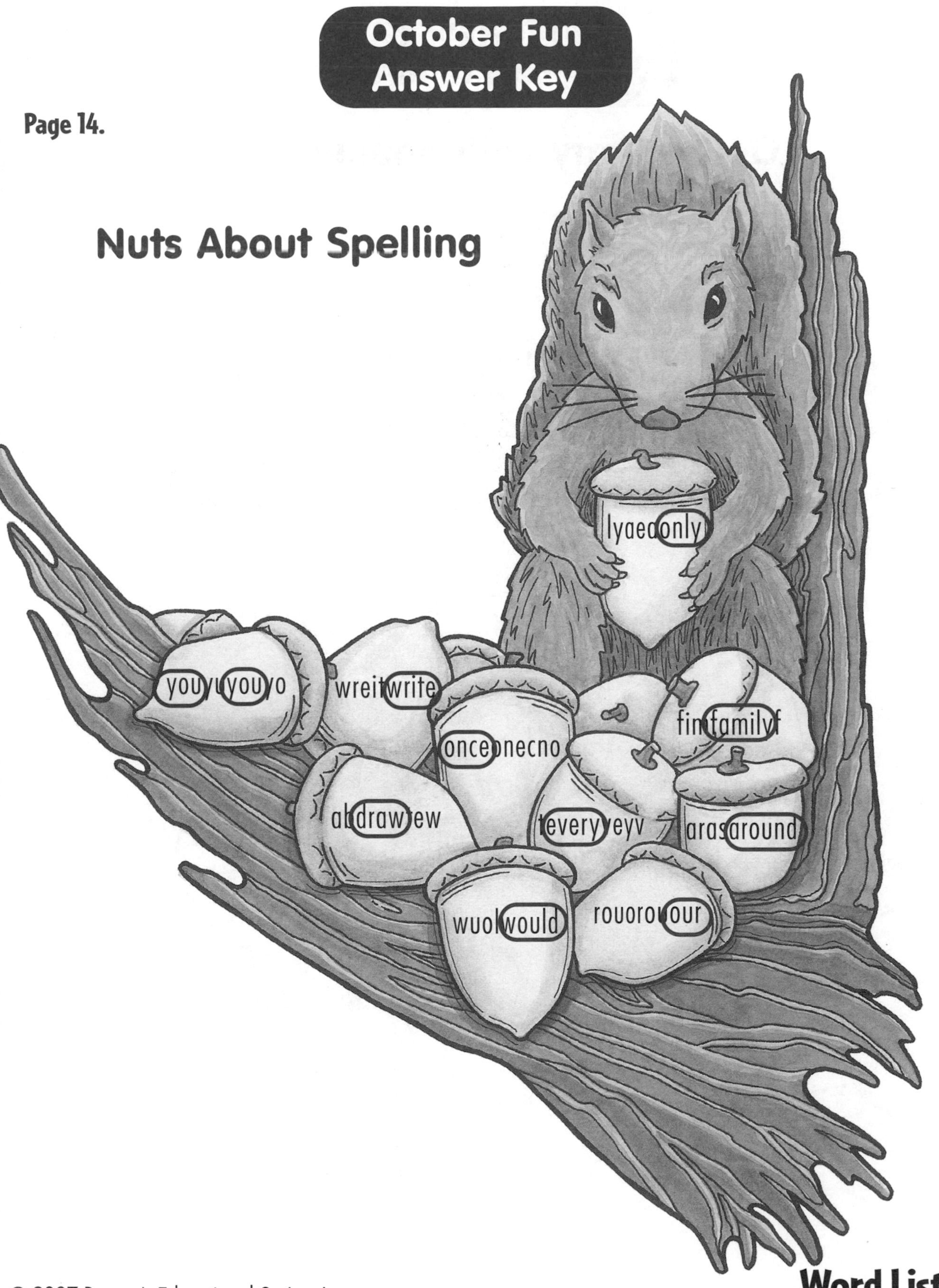

1 2 3 A B C D 1 2 3 A B C 1 2 3 A B C 1 2 3

Word List 2

October Fun Answer Key

Page 15. **Going Batty with Spelling!**

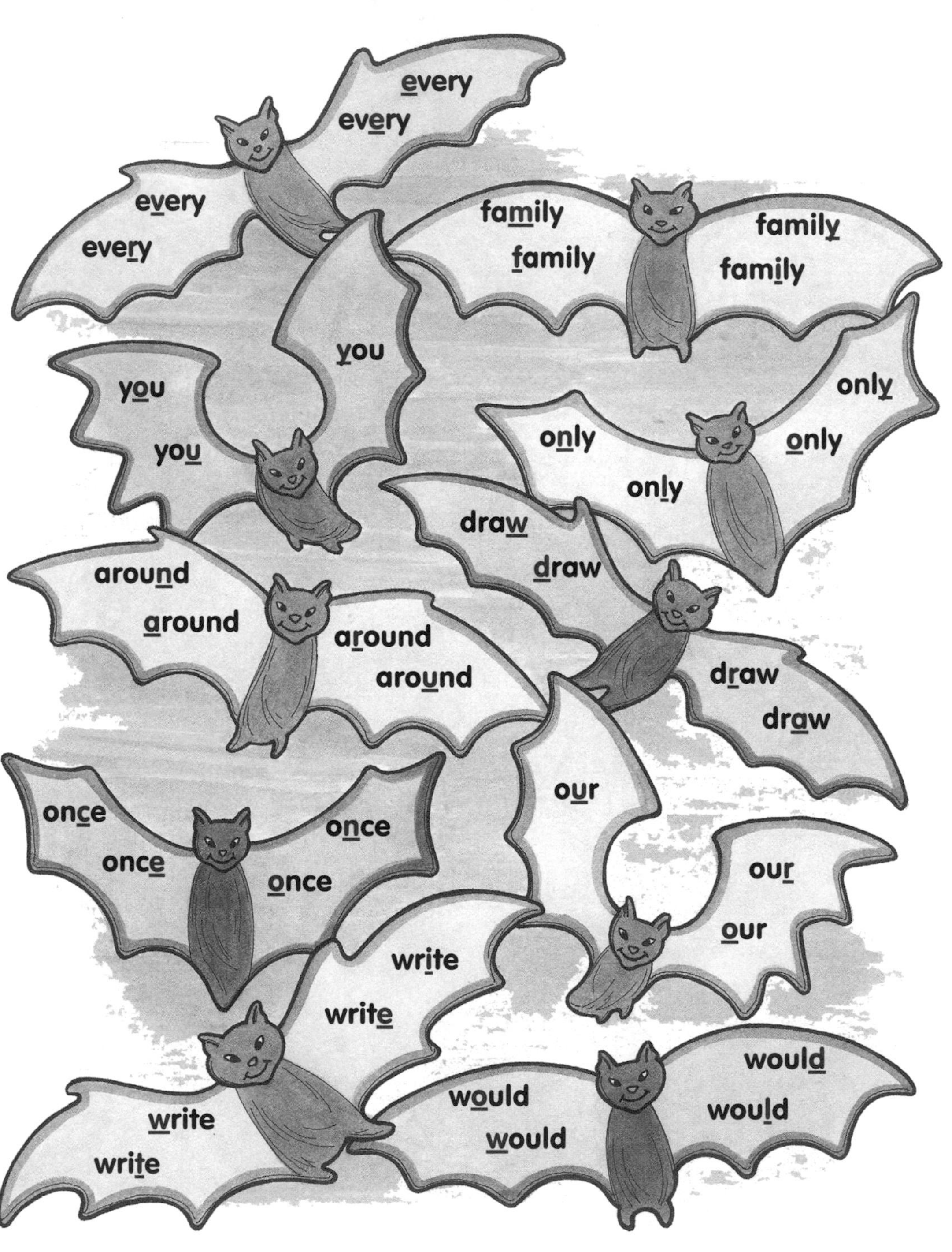

Word List 2

October Fun
Answer Key

Page 16.

An A-mazing Maze!

Word List 2

October Fun
Answer Key

Page 17. **Jack-o'-lantern Spelling**

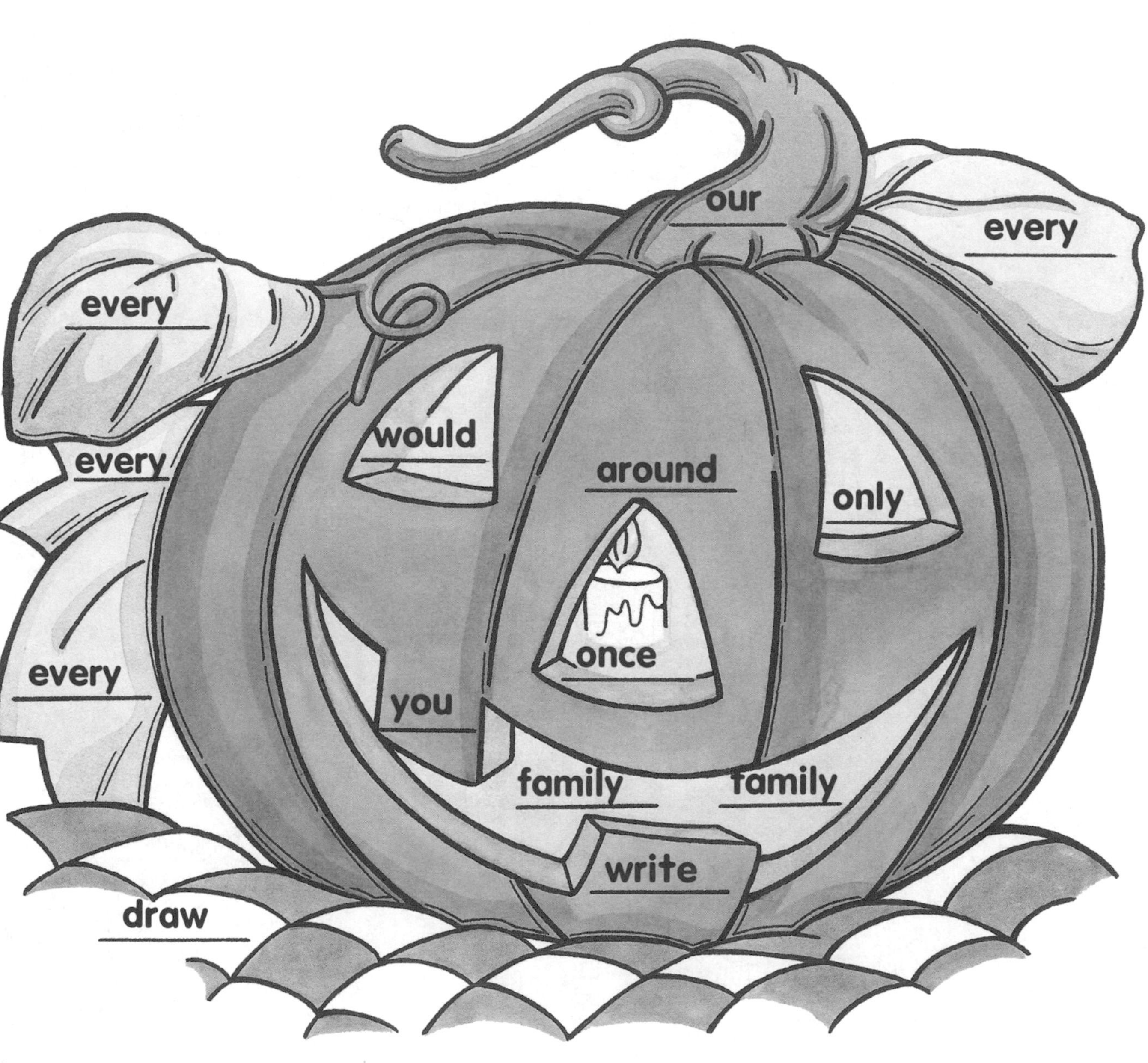

Word List 2

October Fun Answer Key

Page 20.

Five Little Jack-o'-lanterns

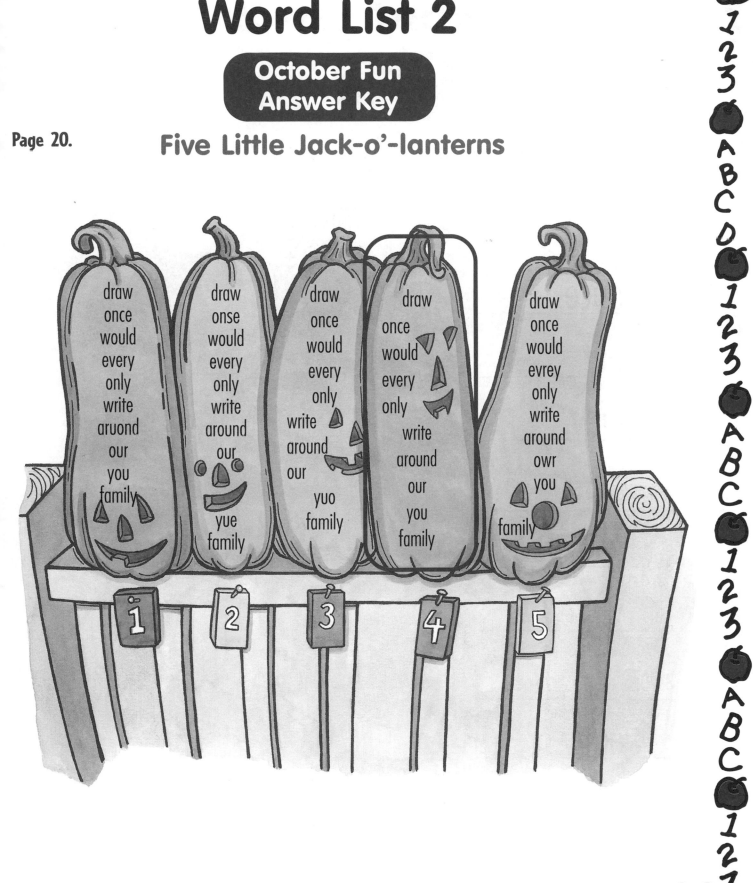

Word List 2

October Fun
Answer Key

Page 21. **Don't Get Spooked Over Spelling!**

1. owl

once

our

only

2. werewolf

would

write

3. Dracula

draw

4. Frankenstein's monster

family

Did you **spell** every **word right?**

Word List 3

November Fun
Answer Key

Page 23.

Shipping Out

Word List 3

November Fun
Answer Key

Page 24.

Plenty to Find

Word List 3

November Fun Answer Key

Page 25.

Oh, Turkey Feathers

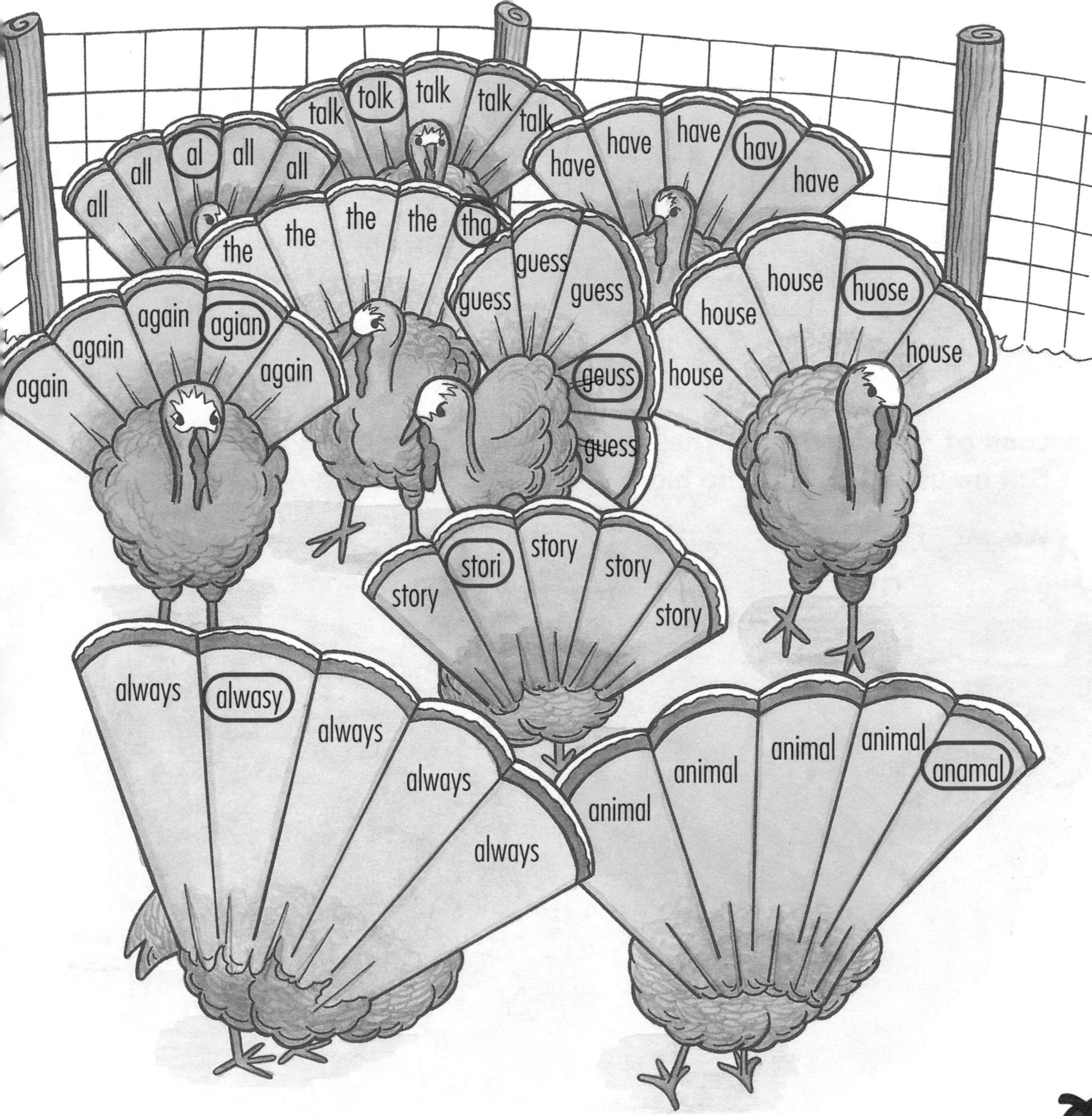

Word List 3

November Fun Answer Key

Page 26.

Word Feast

1. a tale 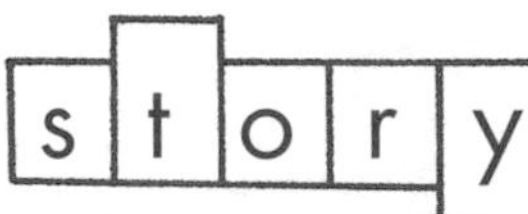

4. to chat 

2. a dog or a cat 

5. every time 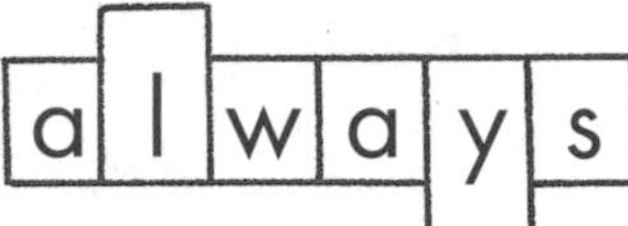

3. a home 

6. every one 

Look at the answers in the boxes. Which two spelling word answers can be used to fill in the blank?

We always **gather together.**

We all **gather together.**

Word List 3

November Fun Answer Key

Page 27.

Bead Codes

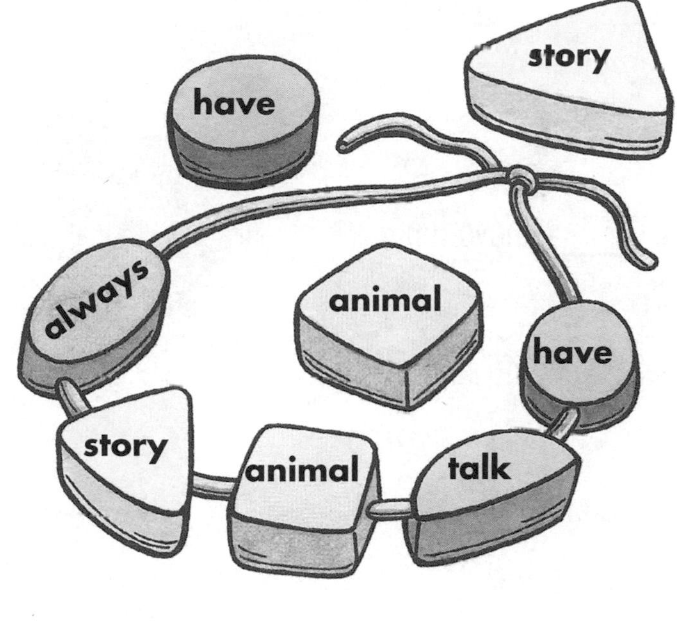

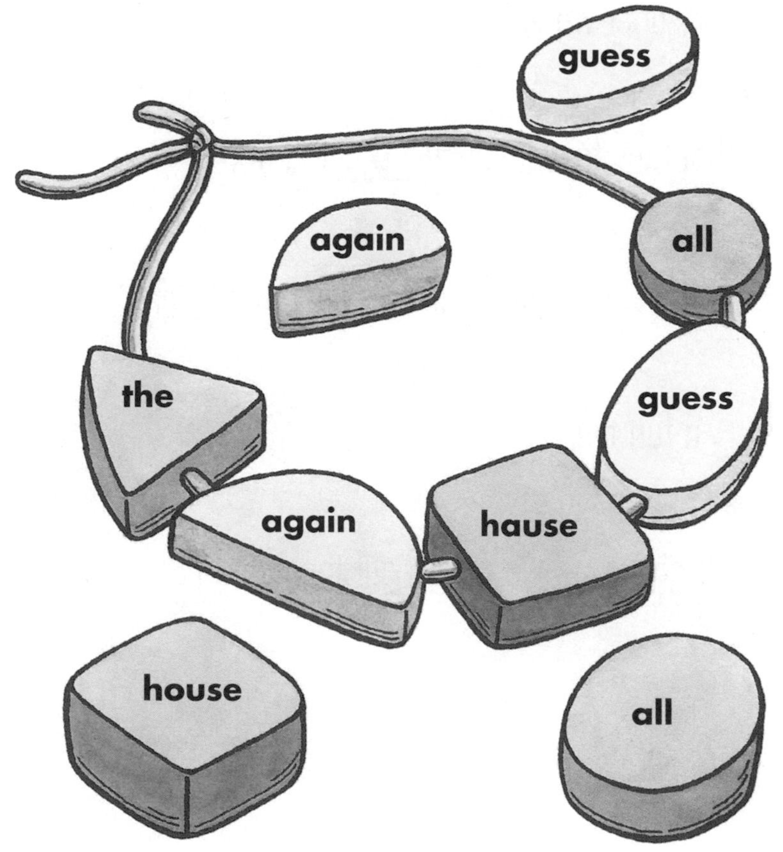

Word List 3

November Fun
Answer Key

Page 28.

Thankful Spelling!

1. On Thanksgiving we alw__a__ys have fun.
   a, i
2. __A__ll the family goes to Grandma's ho__u__se.
   O, A u, o
3. We all sit around the table and ta__l__k.
   o, l
4. Grandma tells us a s__t__ory after we eat.
   h, t
5. Last year she told a story about my favorite anim__a__l, a fox!
   i, a
6. I bet you can g__u__ess we love going to Grandma's for Thanksgiving.
   o, u
7. We alwa__y__s hav__e__ a fun time.
   a, y v, e
8. We can't wait for next Thanksgiving, so we can all get together at Grandma's house ag__a__in.
   a, e

Word List 3

November Fun Answer Key

Page 29.

A Bountiful Harvest!

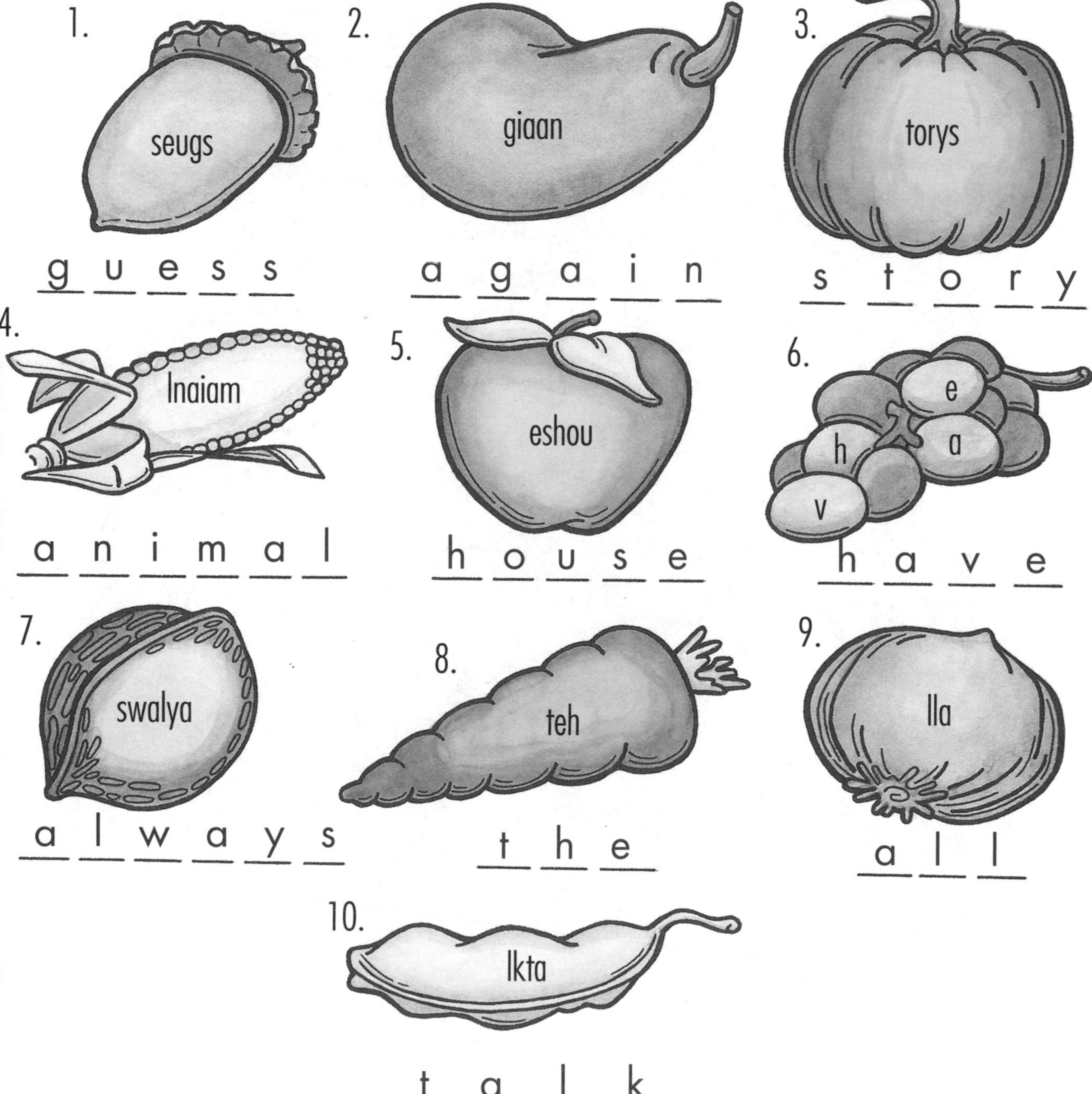

Word List 3

November Fun Answer Key

Page 30.

What a Catch!

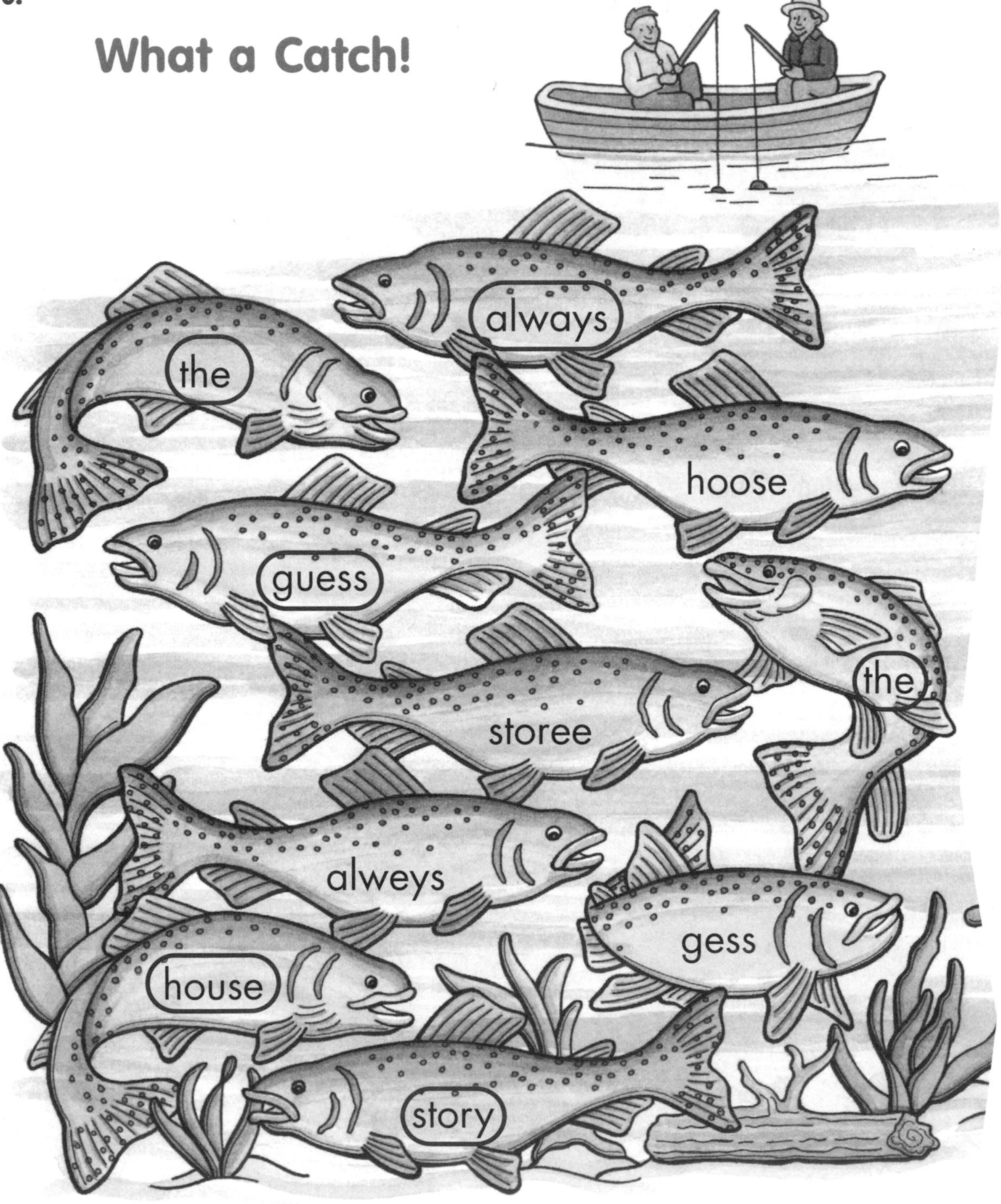

always

the

hoose

guess

the

storee

alweys

gess

house

story

Word List 3

November Fun Answer Key

Page 31. **What a Catch!** (continued)

13 **fish**

Word List 3

November Fun Answer Key

Page 32.

Hats Off to the Pilgrims!

Word List 3

November Fun Answer Key

Page 33.

Harvest Time!

l animal all

k talk

e have the house

y story

s always

n again

Word List 4

December Fun
Answer Key

Page 35.

Happy Holidays!

1. how **2.** are **3.** there **4.** eye **5.** kind **6.** any **7.** they

8. about **9.** know **10.** their **11.** answer

Page 37.

Colorful Candy Canes

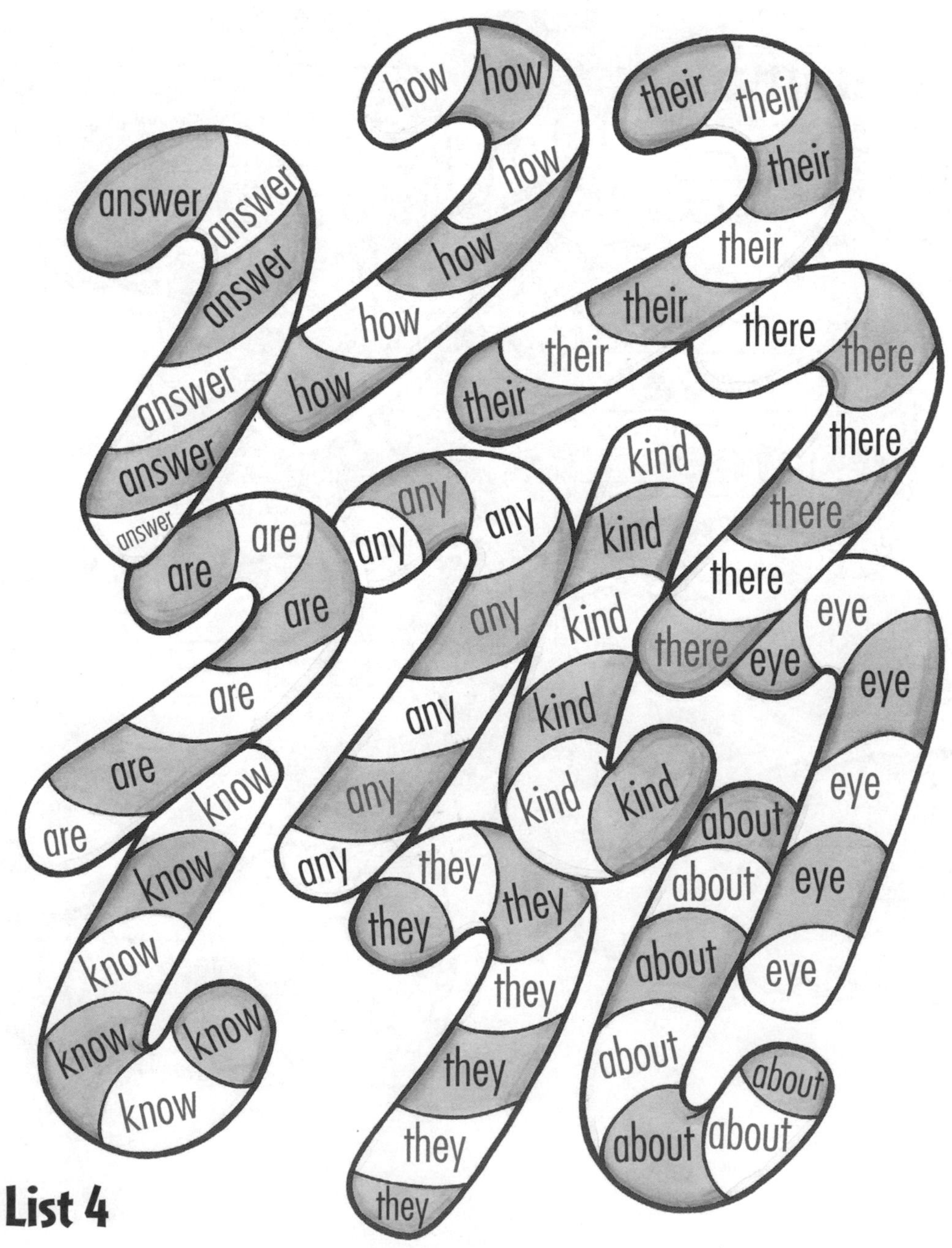

Word List 4

December Fun Answer Key

Page 39.

Happy Hanukkah!

Word List 4

December Fun Answer Key

Page 40.

Stocking Stuffers

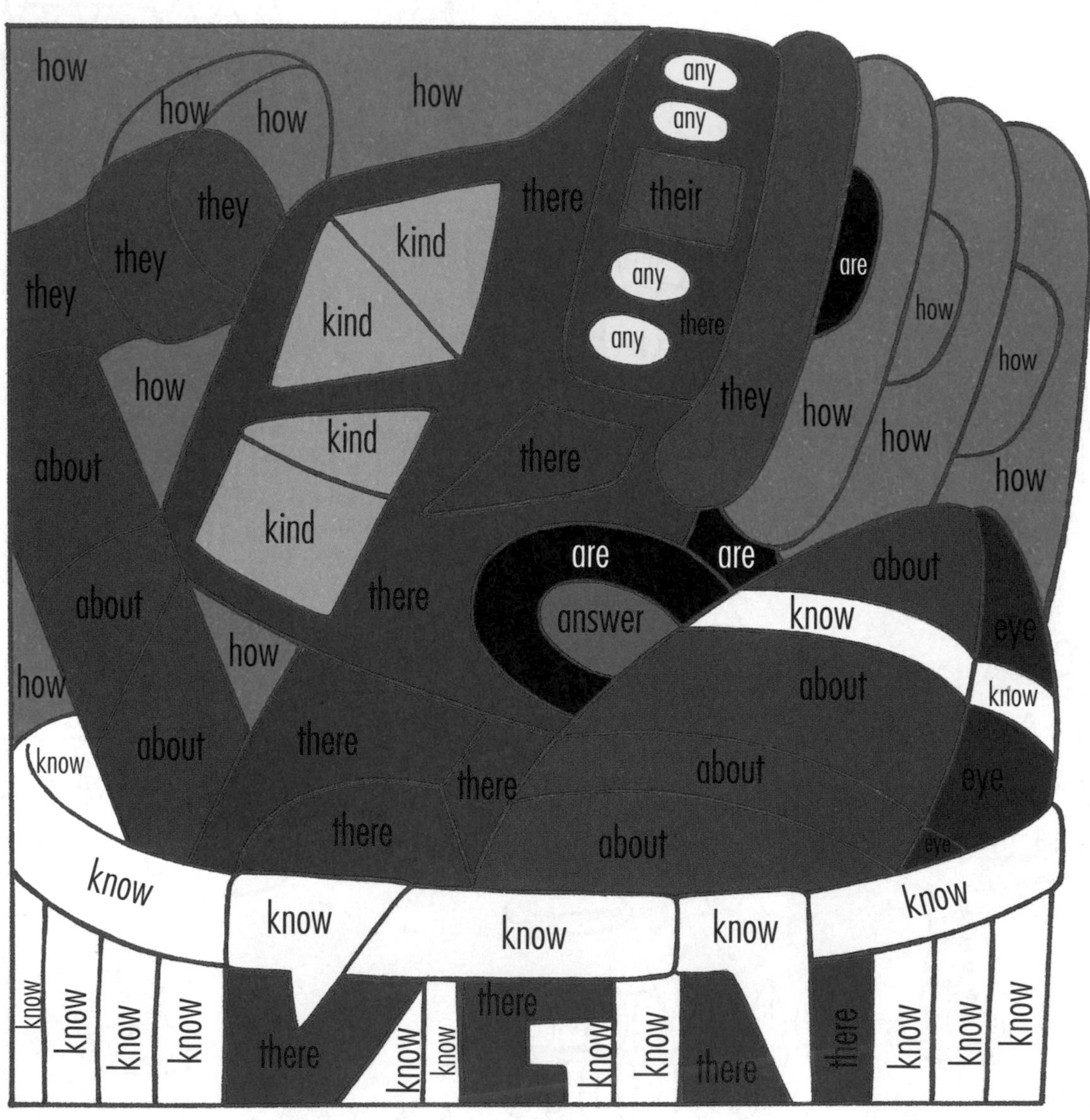

Page 41.

Where's Rudolph?

Path 2

Word List 4

December Fun
Answer Key

Page 42.

Holiday Word Sort

Word List 4

December Fun Answer Key

Page 43.

Jingle Bells

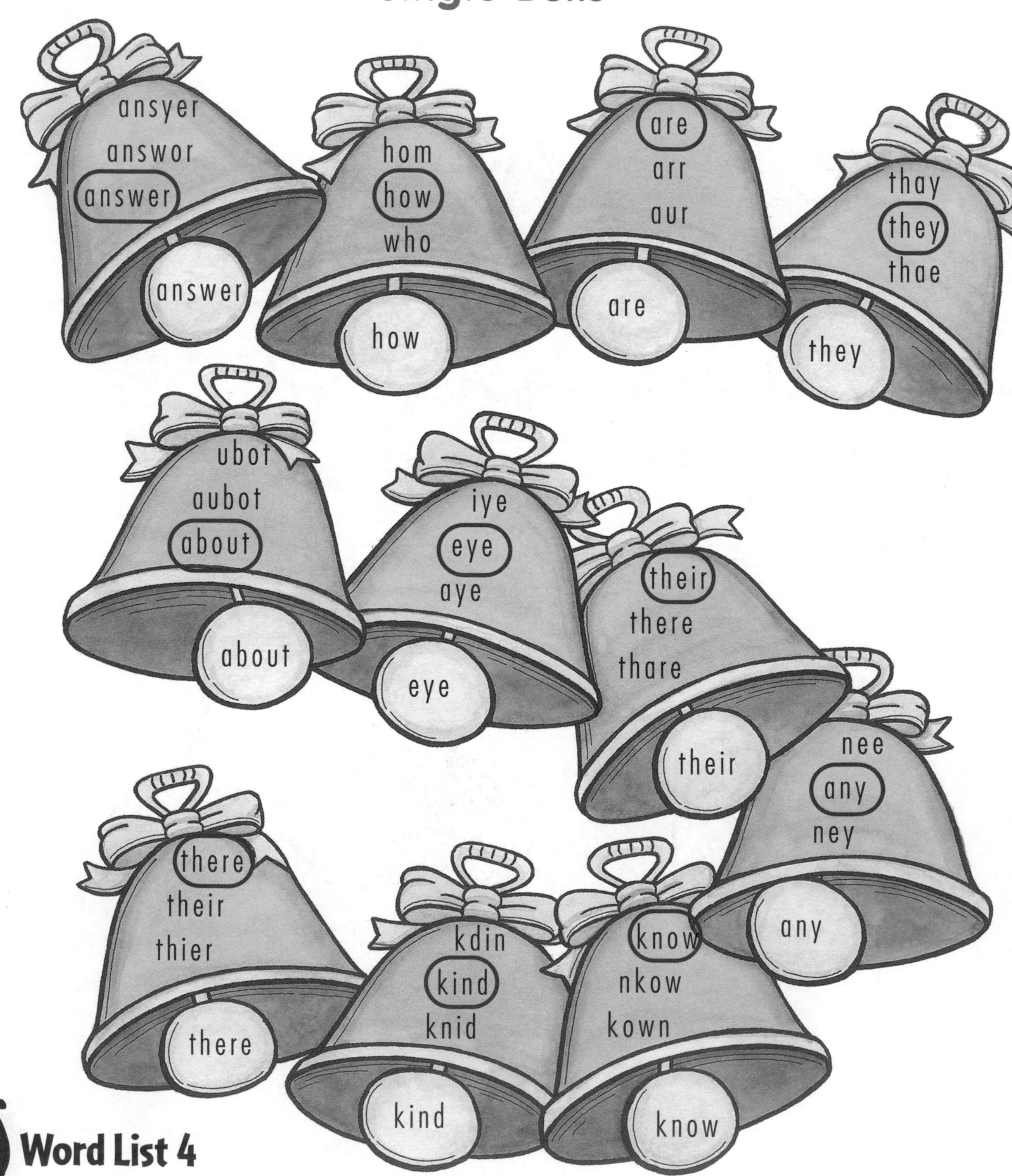

Word List 4

December Fun Answer Key

Page 44.

All Aboard!

Riddles
1. kind good and nice
2. any one out of many
3. there a place
4. their belonging to them
5. about almost
6. know to think in your mind
7. how tell which way
8. eye used to see
9. they them
10. are We______ all happy.
11. answer give a reply to a question

Word List 5

January Fun Answer Key

Page 46.

Brr! It's January

find = **find** fond

school = skul **school**

good = godo **good**

soon = **soon** soot

put = pun **put**

says = sez **says**

said = **said** siad

saw = **saw** sow

shoes = shose **shoes**

great = **great** graet

Page 47.

Let It Snow!!

Word List 5

January Fun Answer Key

Page 49.

Where's My Hat?

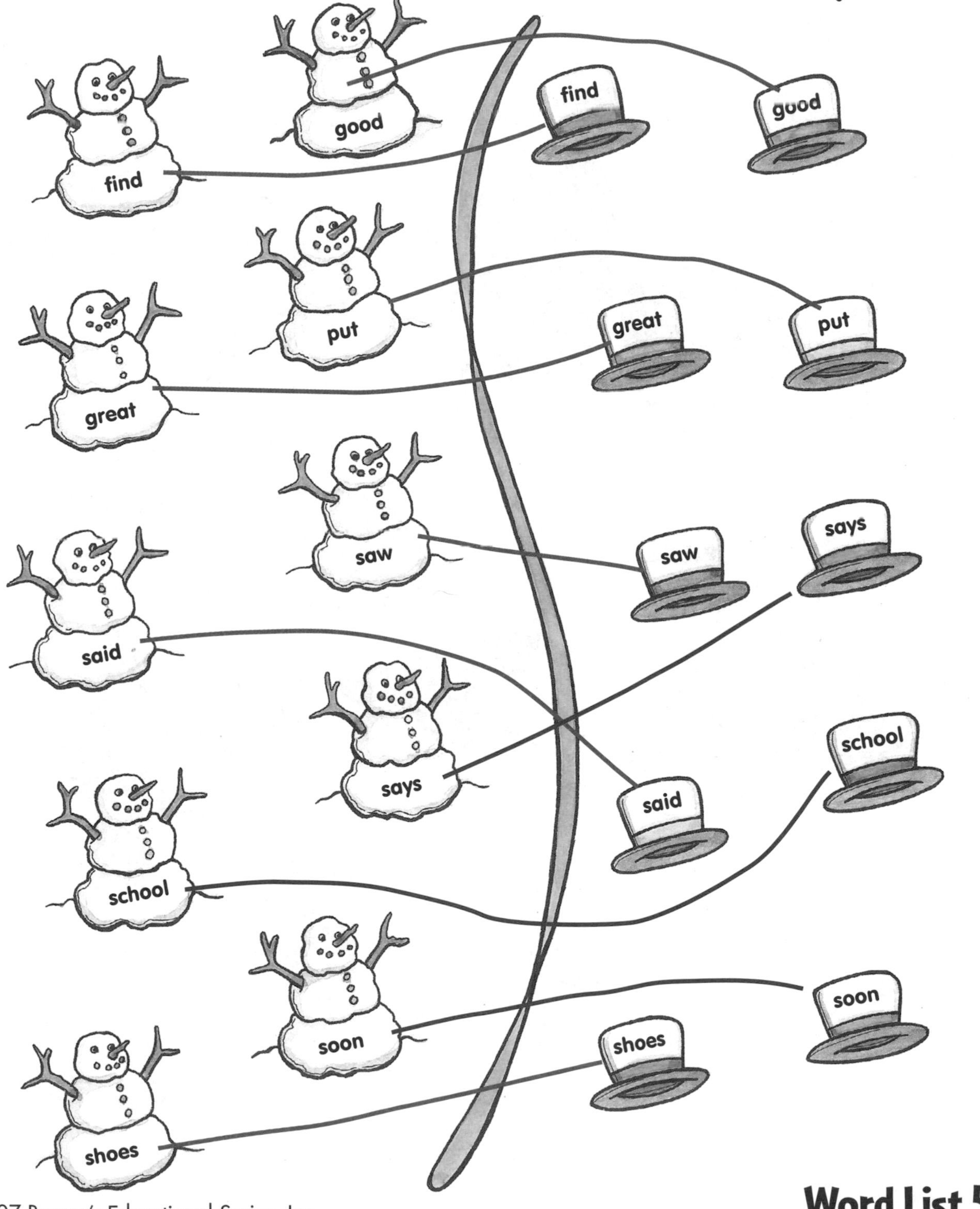

Word List 5

January Fun Answer Key

Page 50.

A Polar Wonderland

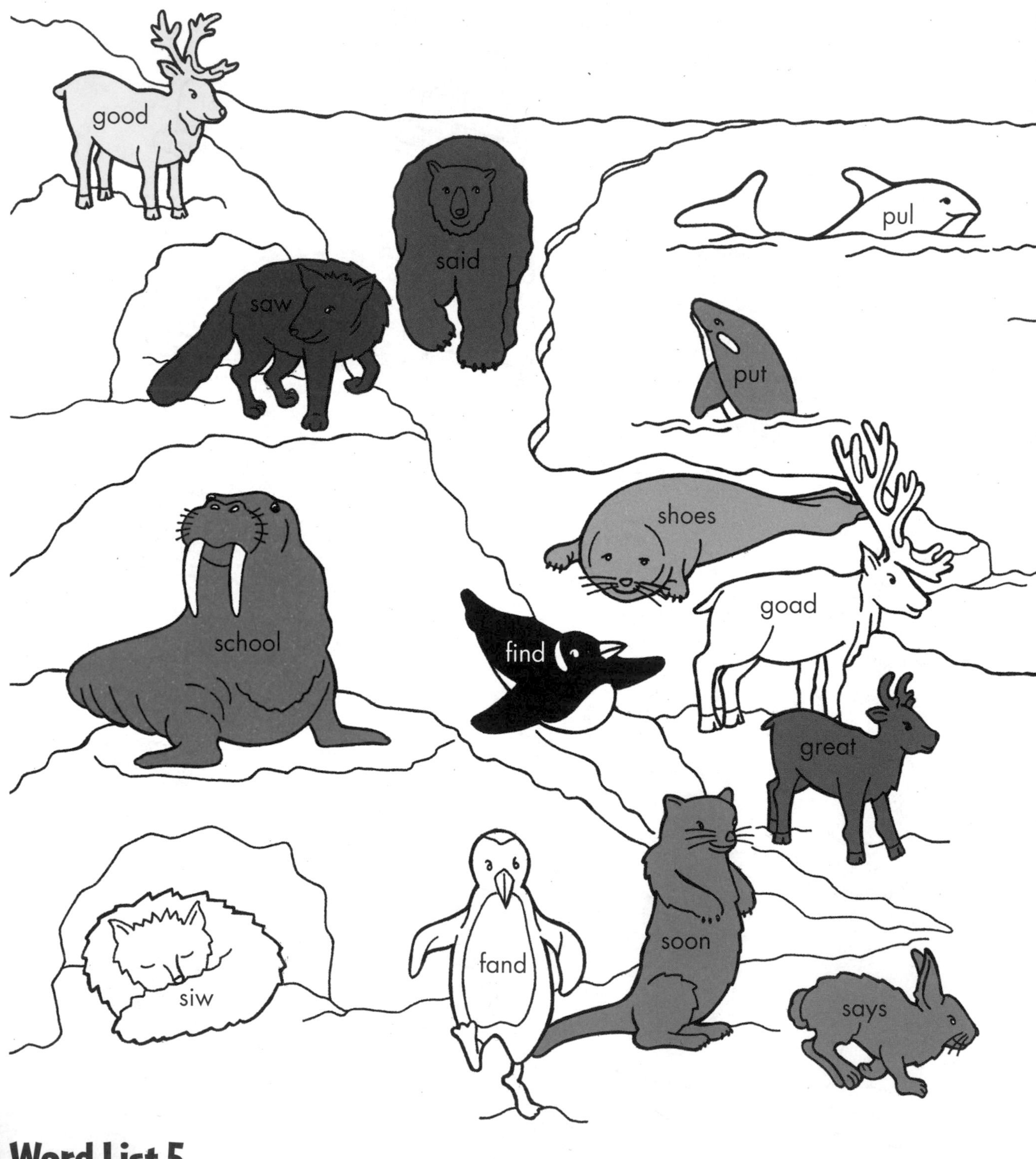

Word List 5

January Fun Answer Key

Page 51.

A Polar Wonderland (continued)

Word List 5

January Fun
Answer Key

Page 52.

Pretty Little Snowflakes

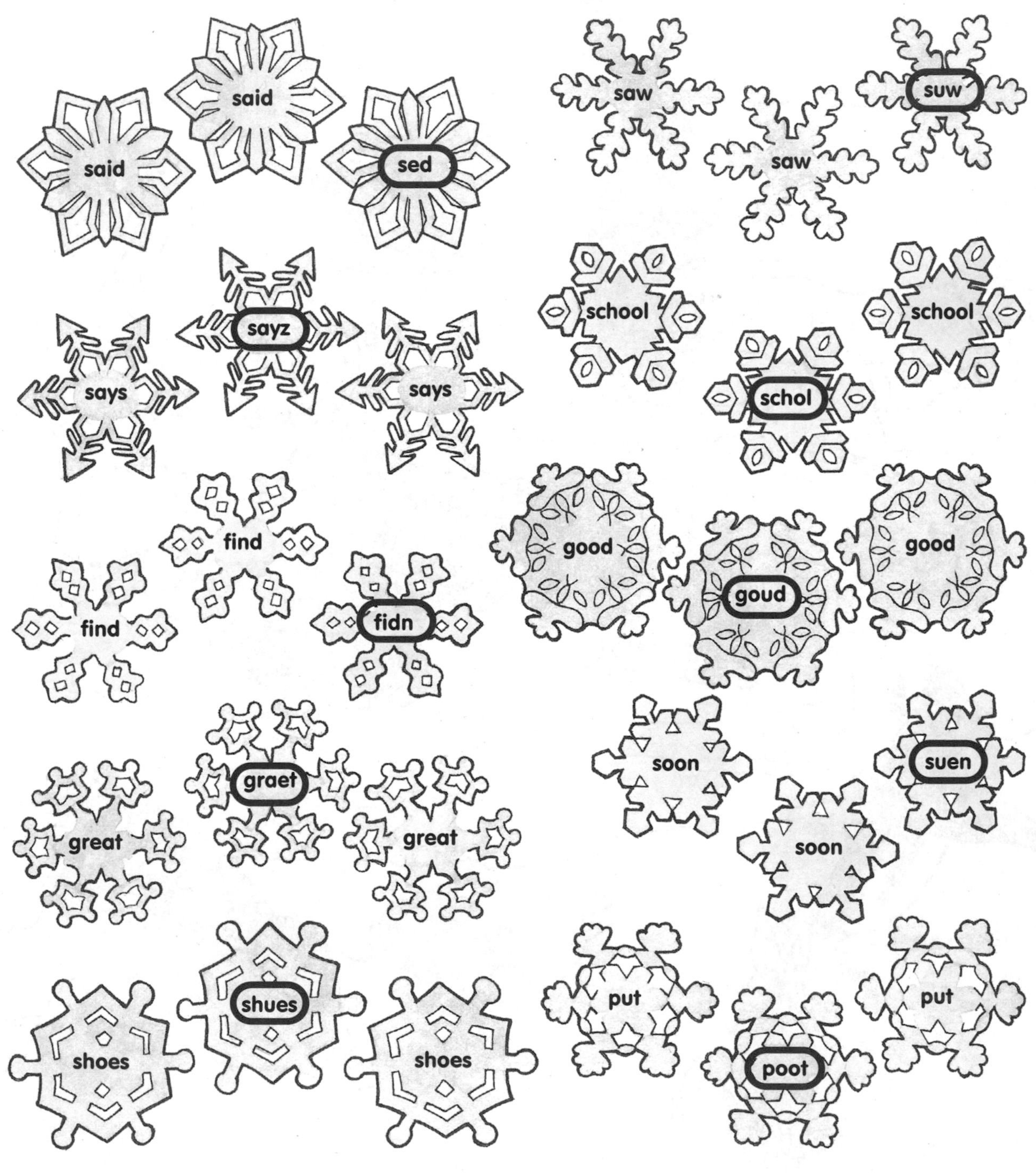

Word List 5

January Fun Answer Key

Oh What Fun!

Page 53.

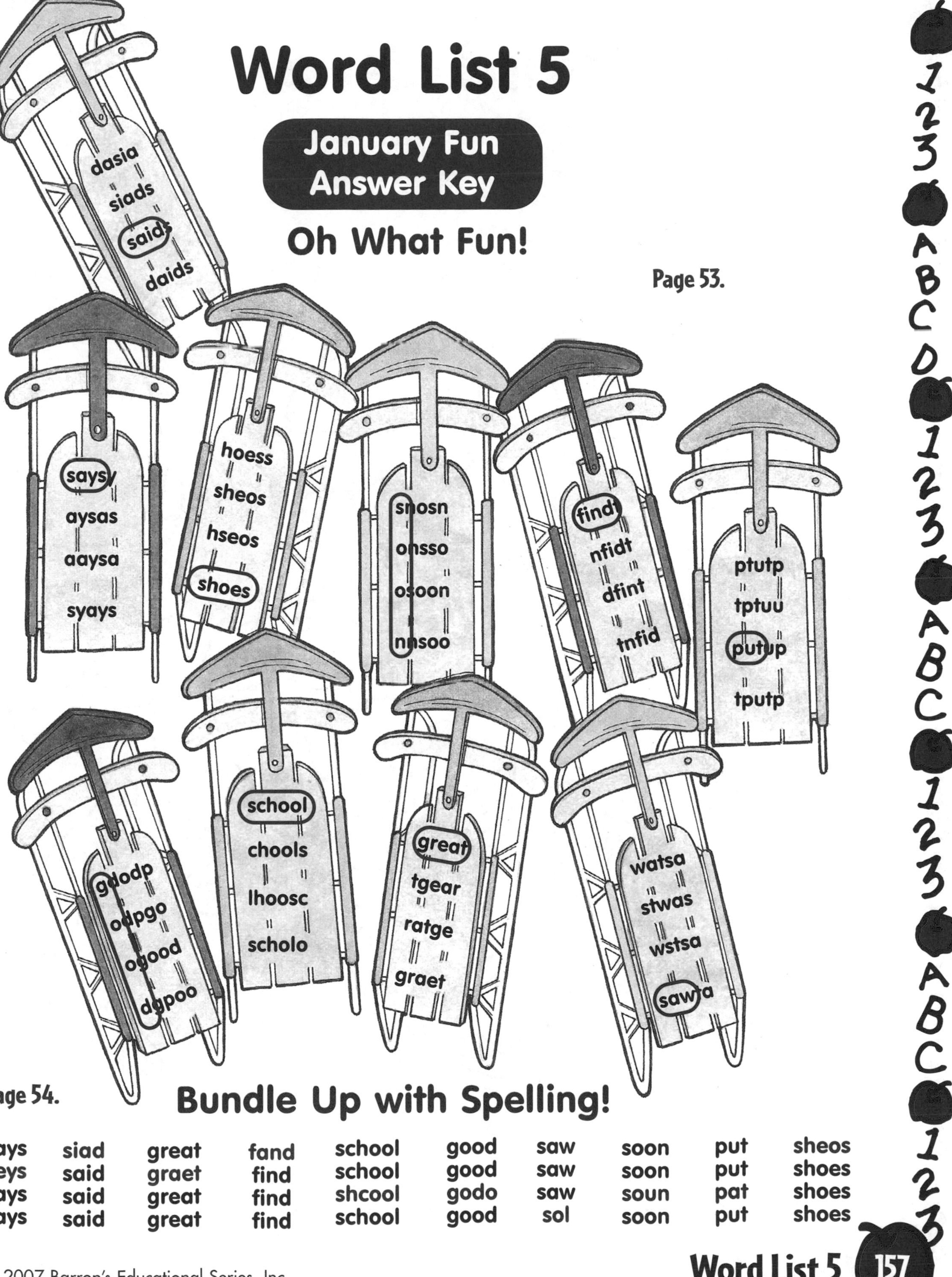

Page 54.

Bundle Up with Spelling!

says	siad	great	fand	school	good	saw	soon	put	sheos
seys	said	graet	find	school	good	saw	soon	put	shoes
says	said	great	find	shcool	godo	saw	soun	pat	shoes
says	said	great	find	school	good	sol	soon	put	shoes

Word List 5

January Fun Answer Key

Page 55.

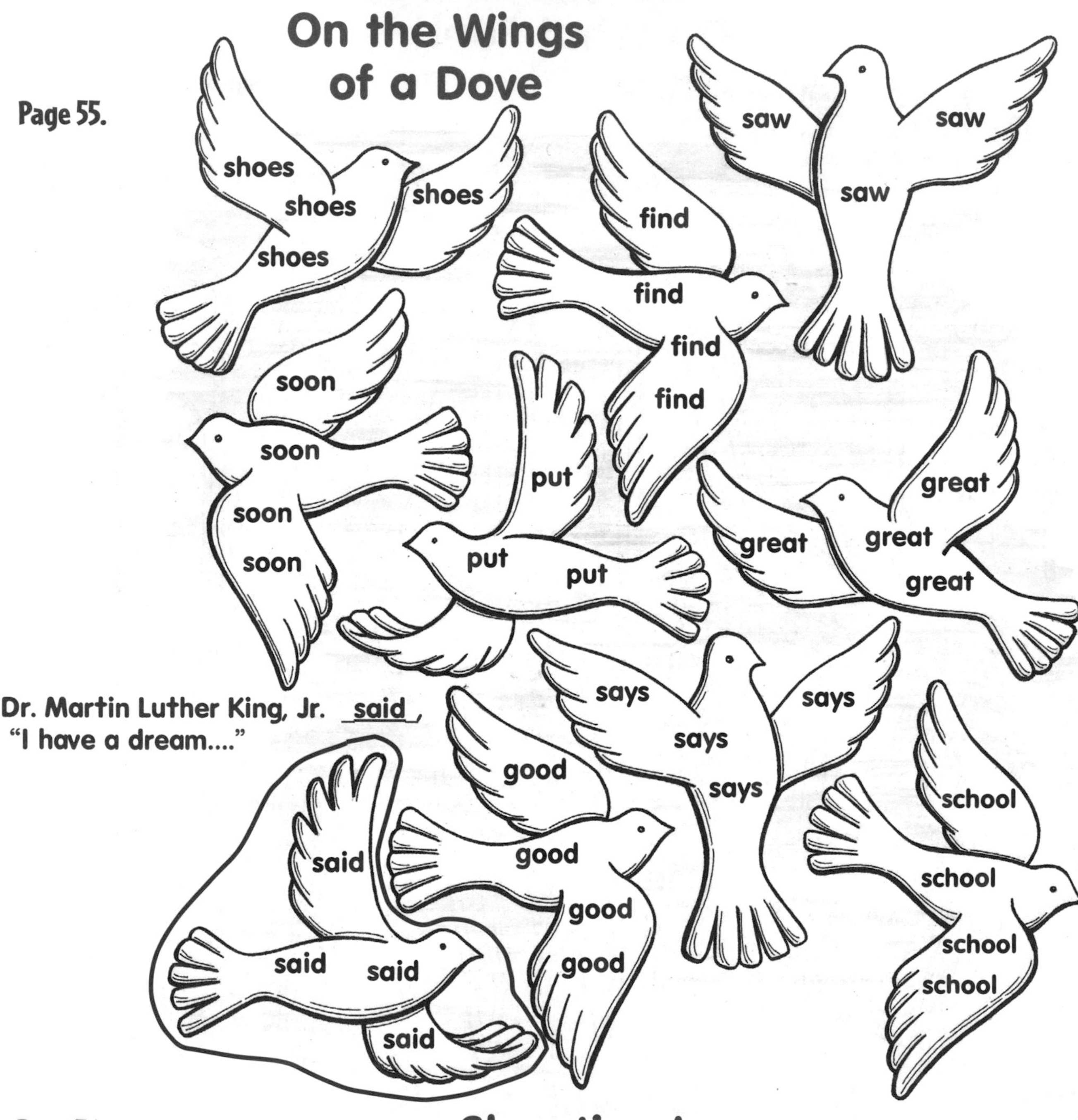

Page 56.

Showtime!

Answers
1. soon 2. school 3. saw 4. sa 5. great 6. shoes 7. put 8. find 9. good 10. ai

Word List 6

February Fun Answer Key

Page 58.

Groundhog Spelling Math

1. mother **2.** by **3.** buy **4.** movc **5.** was **6.** circle **7.** brother **8.** wanl

Page 60.

Who's Who? What's What?

Lincoln **1.** circle **2.** watch **3.** by **4.** saw **5.** want

Washington **1.** my **2.** mother **3.** brother **4.** move **5.** buy

Page 61.

A Priceless Gift!

The Gift

I wont to bey my muther a gift for Valentine's Day. I think she would like a wutch. A watch costs a lot. I will ask mi big bruther to help me buy a watch for mother. My brother has a job. He will help me buy a gift. Mother will be happy with her gift. But she will be even more pleased that we went together to get it.

1. want **2.** buy **3.** mother **4.** watch **5.** my **6.** brother

Word List 6

February Fun
Answer Key

Page 62.

Code Jewels

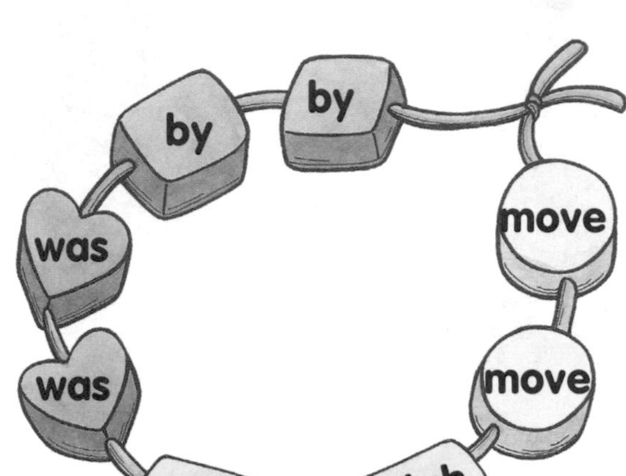

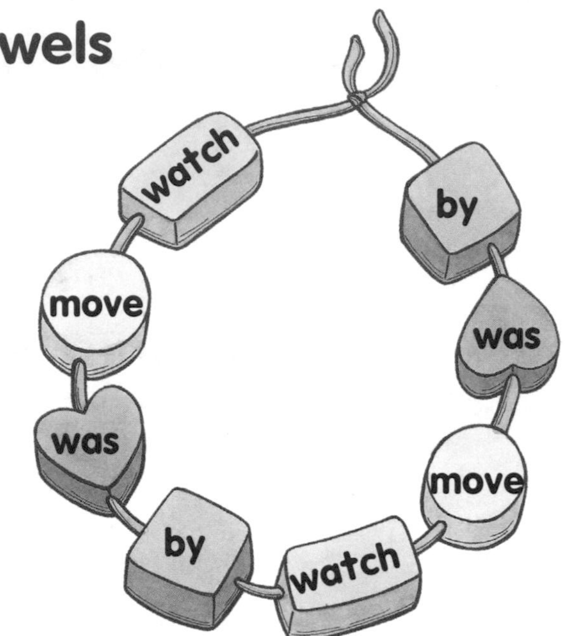

Page 63.

Get to the Heart of It!

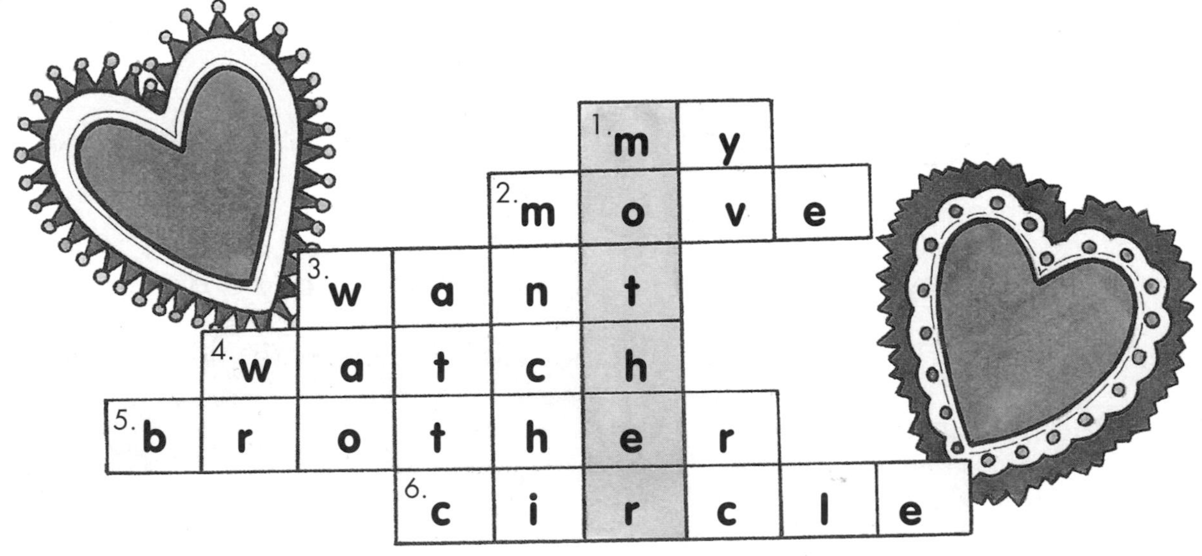

I love my ___mother___ .

Word List 6

February Fun Answer Key

Page 64.

Rosy Endings

r—brother, mother **e**—move, circle **t**—want **y**—buy, by, my **s**—was **h**—watch

Page 65.

Which Way to the Tarts?

PATH 1.

Page 66.

Take Aim at Spelling

cel**circle**r m**by**uthrb

omt**mother**m v**move**lcir

ybury**buy** **brother**yr

wsat**was**tc wos**my**rle

anwn**want**n tch**watch**rt

Page 67.

Put Your Heart Into Spelling

Answers

1. brother 2. move 3. mother 4. my 5. by 6. was 7. circle 8. buy 9. want 10. watch

Word List 7

March Fun Answer Key

Page 69.

Lions or Lambs?

Lion	Lamb
lok	away
liun	took
toi	to
laf	as
	ball
	food

Page 70.

Up and Away!

to, lion, as, away, look, ball, laugh, took, lion, food, too

11 kites

Page 71.

Where's Me Pots of Gold?

1. s **2.** ll **3.** ugh **4.** ok **5.** ood **6.** ok **7.** ay **8.** on **9.** o **10.** oo

Pages 72–73.

Word Rainbows

Each word written in red, orange, yellow, green, blue, indigo-blue purple, and violet-purple:

as, laugh, to, away, lion, too, food, look, took, ball

Page 74.

No Blarney!

as, laugh, to, away, lion, too, food, look, took, ball
written repeatedly around noted shamrocks

Word List 7

March Fun
Answer Key

Page 75.

Oh, What a Parade!

Word List 7

March Fun Answer Key

Page 76.

What Luck!

Lucky Leprechaun

I tried (to) catch a leprechaun, so I hid behind a tree. When he ran by, I reached out (to) grab him, but in a flash and with a (laugh) he dashed (away). I don't know how it happened, because (as) I grabbed at him, I felt I had him good, but when I (took) a closer (look), all I had was his little green coat. What luck!

Page 77.

St. Patrick's Day Surprise!

1. Look **2.** to **3.** look **4.** laugh **5.** too **6.** ball

Page 78.

Derby Daze

ase—**as**, liun—**lion**, bol—**ball**, uway—**away**, ti—**to**, foad—**food**, tou—**too**, tok—**took**, loek—**look,** luagh—**laugh**

Page 79.

A Lucky Kiss!

1. laugh **2.** Food **3.** ball **4.** Look

5. lion **6.** away **7.** too **8.** took

9. as **10.** to

Word List 8

April Fun Answer Key

Page 81.

Umbrella Time!

one	**do**	**who**	**old**	**down**	**where**	**does**	**of**	**won**	**oh**
one	do	who	old	down	where	does	of	won	oh
one	do	who	old	down	where	does	of	won	oh
one	*do*	*who*	*old*	*down*	*where*	*does*	*of*	*won*	*oh*

Page 82. (see p. 166)

Egg Hunt

Page 83.

Colored Eggs

does

Page 86.

Egg Sort

Floppy Bunny—2
do, oh, of
Hoppy Bunny—3
who, old, won, one
Loppy Bunny—4
does, down
Cloppy Bunny—5
where

Hoppy Bunny **won** the contest.

Word List 8

April Fun
Answer Key

Egg Hunt

Page 82.

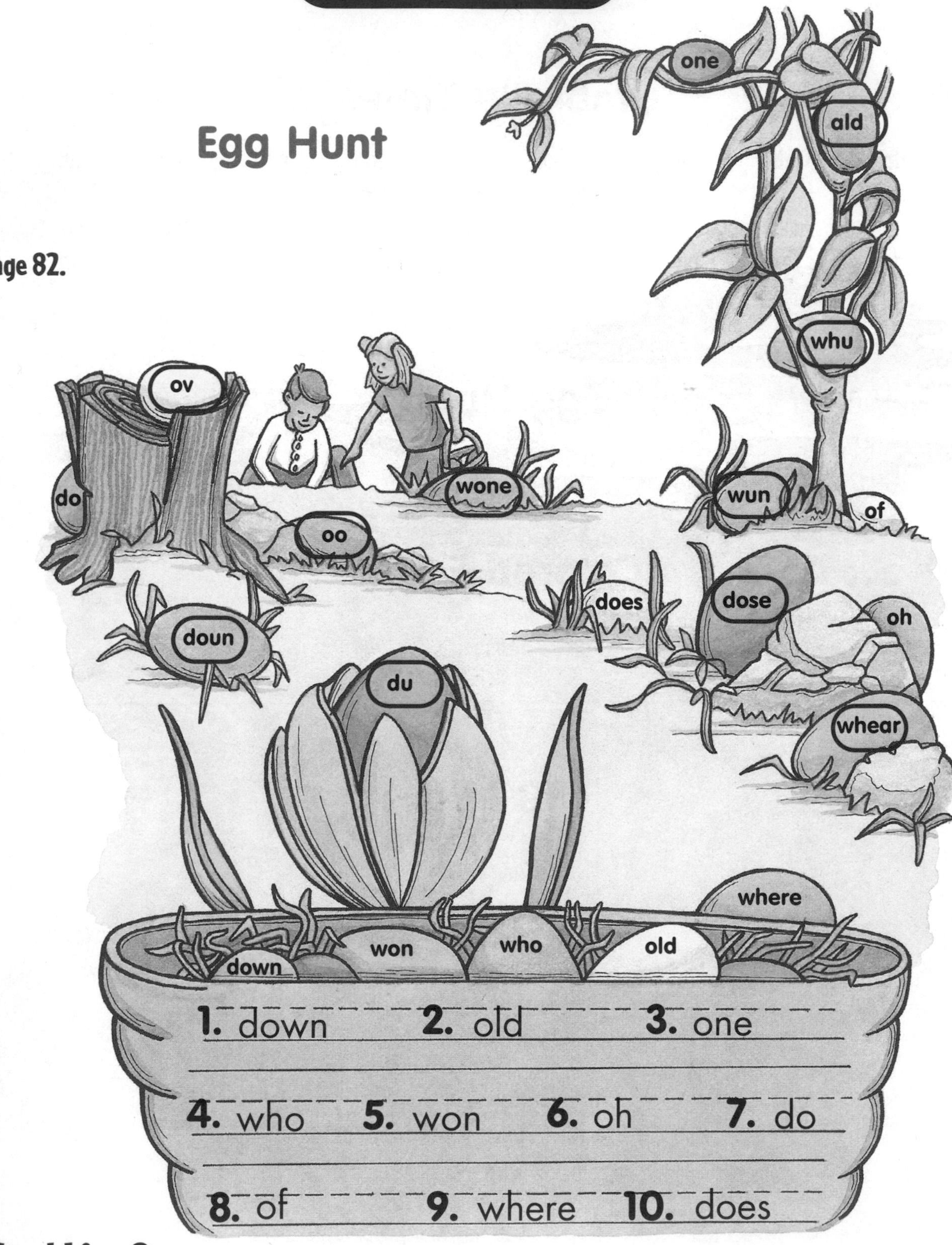

Word List 8

April Fun Answer Key

Page 87.

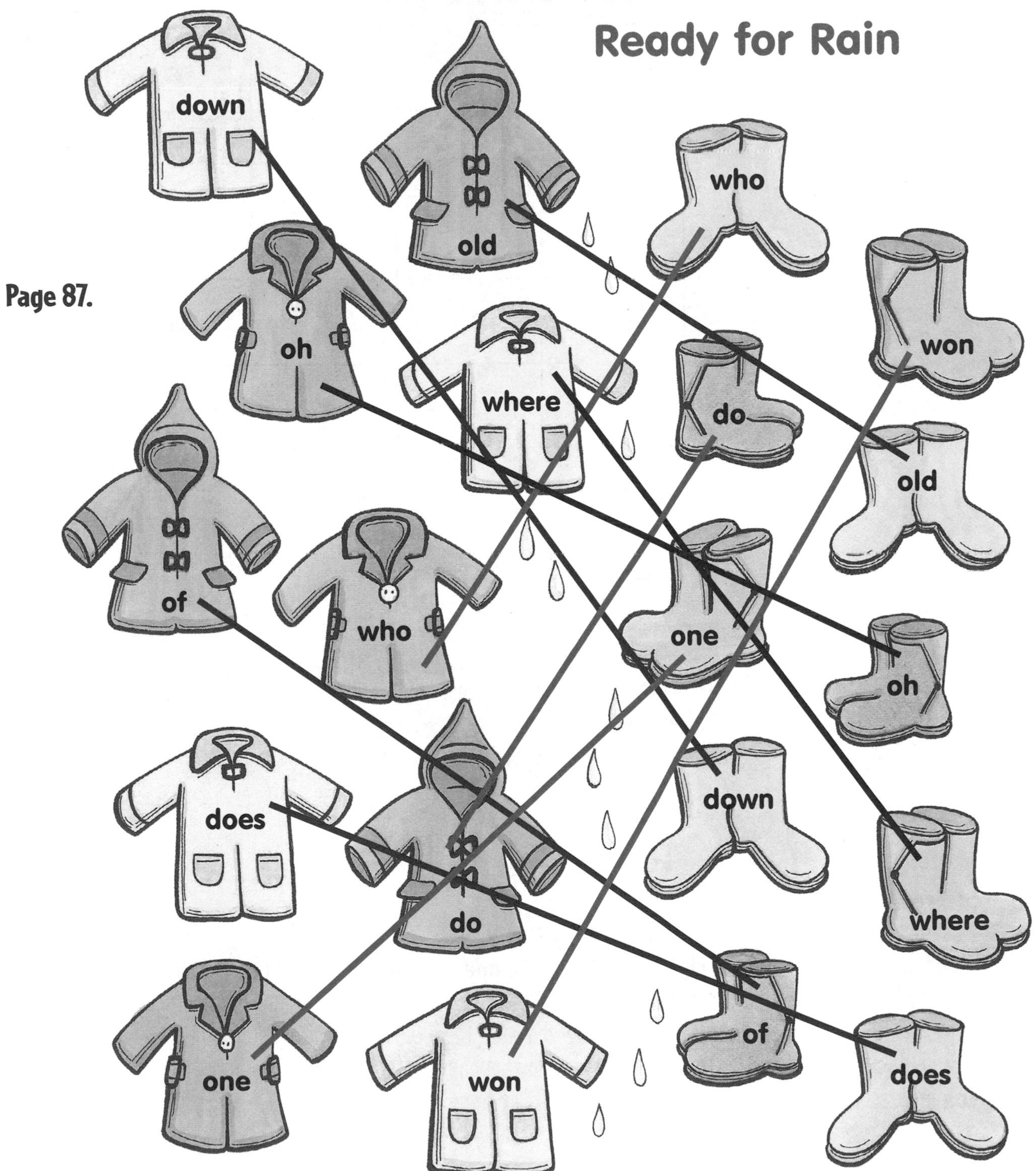

Word List 8

April Fun Answer Key

Page 88. **Puzzled**

	1. d	o	w	n
		2. w	h	o
	3. d	o	e	s
4. w	h	e	r	e
	5. o	n	e	

Where did Easter Bunny hide my basket?

Page 89.

A Dandy Sort

Beginning with d—do, does, down
Beginning with o—oh, of, old, one
Beginning with w—where, who, won
Ending with o—do, who,
Ending with n—down, won

Page 91.

Party Time

A Birthday Party

One **of** my friends has a little brother. His brother will be **one** year **old**. He is having a birthday party. My friend asked me to come to the party, but I don't know **where** he lives.
I hope my mom **does**. He said he lives **down** by the lake. There are only three houses there, so it can't be too hard to find. **Oh** boy! I hope we play fun games. The last party I went to I **won** a prize. **Who** knows, maybe I will win again. I like to go to parties. **Do** you like to go to parties, too?

Word List 9

May Fun Answer Key

Page 93.

The Very Wordy Caterpillers

love, many, both　through, lose　because, very　book, money, walk

Page 94.

Flower Power

1. because **2.** very **3.** many **4.** book **5.** money **6.** walk **7.** love **8.** through **9.** both **10.** lose

Page 95.

Spring into Math Spelling

1. lose **2.** many **3.** book **4.** love **5.** very **6.** both **7.** through **8.** lose

Pages 96–97.

Welcome to My Garden

Write the following word list words written repeatedly around the flower:

1. lose **2.** many **3.** book **4.** love **5.** very **6.** both **7.** through **8.** lose

Page 98.

All Abuzz

through	throg	thrugh	(through)
lose	loos	(lose)	luse
many	mony	(many)	mnoy
very	(very)	vory	vary
both	buth	(both)	boht
because	becos	becase	(because)
walk	(walk)	walke	wakl
money	munny	(money)	monee
book	(book)	booc	bok
love	levo	(love)	lov

Word List 9

May Fun
Answer Key

Page 99.

Where's My Lunch?

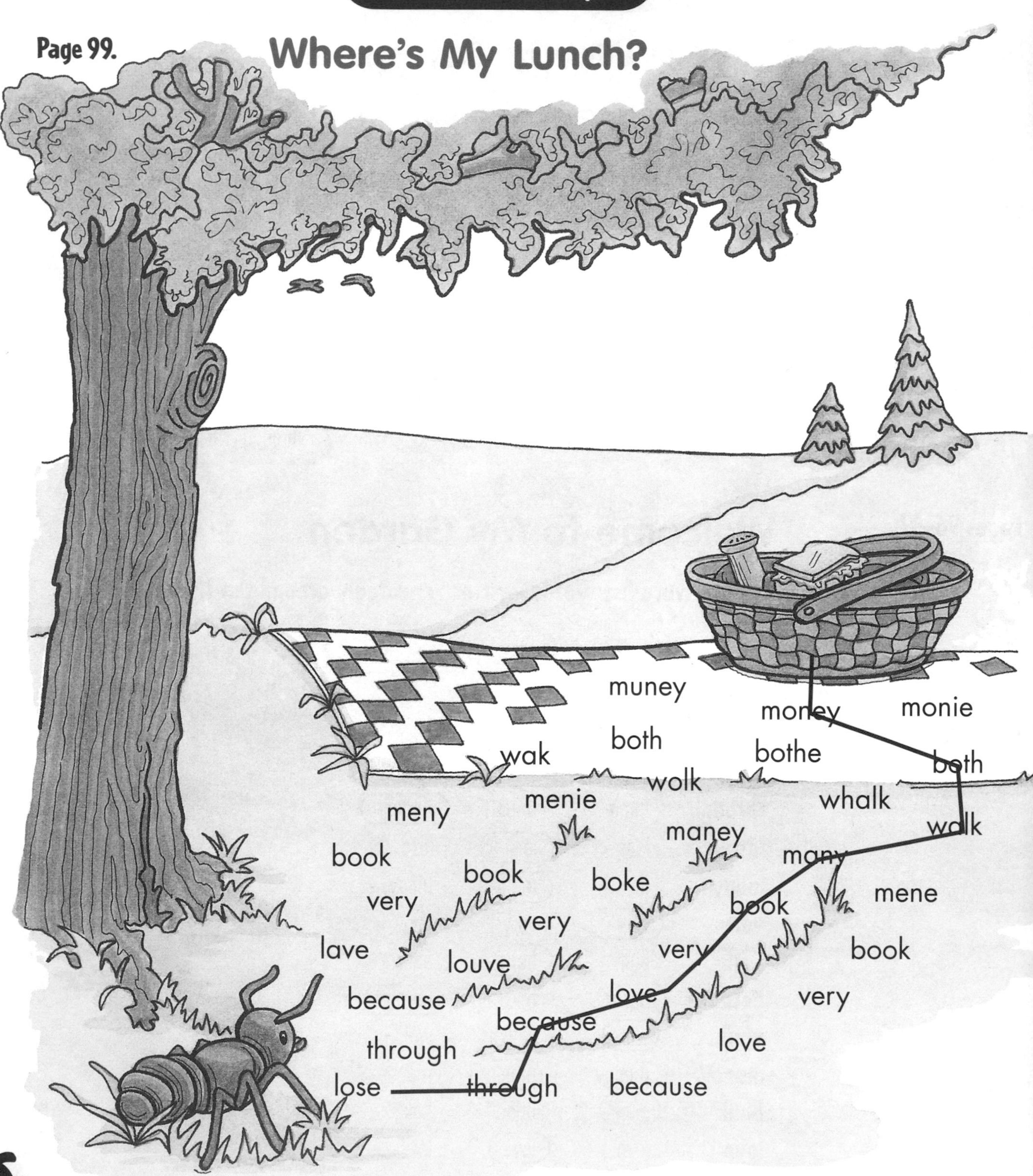

Word List 9

May Fun
Answer Key

Pages 100–101.

Here Comes the Sun!

money	love	both	through	because	many	lose	very	walk	book
money	love	both	through	because	many	lose	very	walk	book
money	love	both	through	because	many	lose	very	walk	book
money	love	both	through	because	many	lose	very	walk	book
money	love	both	through	because	many	lose	very	walk	book
money			through	because					
			through	because					
			through	because					

Page 103.

Spring into Action

Answers

1. lose 2. through 3. money

1. because 2. love 3. very 4. book 5. many 6. walk 7. both

Word List 10

June Fun Answer Key

Page 105.

Fun-in-the-Sun Codes

1. could **2.** some **3.** new **4.** were **5.** what **6.** come **7.** now **8.** color **9.** water **10.** climb

Page 108.

Dig Into Spelling!

climb, color, were, come, what, new, water, now, some, could

Page 109.

Have a Ball!

climb, color, were, come, what, new, water, now, some, could
traced and written 3 times

Page 110.

Hidden Treasure

Where Could It Be?

The **water** at the beach feels great! The sun does, too. Grab your suit and a towel, and **come** and have **some** fun! The sea is the perfect **color** of blue. It is so clear you never can tell **what** you might see. **Climb** aboard a boat. It doesn't matter if it's old or **new**. Go for a ride out on the waves as if you **were** a pirate. Look out over the sea with your spyglass to your eye. **Now** just where was it that you hid your silver and your gold?

Could, water, come, some, color, what, Climb, new, were, Now

Word List 10

June Fun Answer Key

Page 111.

Toasty Word Shapes

Page 112.

Set Up Camp!

1. whut **2.** com **3.** neew **4.** som **5.** cuold
6. naw **7.** werr **8.** culer **9.** woter **10.** clim

Word List 10

June Fun Answer Key

Page 113.

A Glow in the Dark!

were, were, come, could, climb, some, color, new, now, what

Page 114.

Don't Tip Your Canoe!

no**could**t sume**now** **water**anr lim**climb** r**color**lor rer**were**w
so**some**m **what**nrtw wnw**new**n m**come**mc

Page 115.

Time to Show What You Know!

Camp Out

In the summer my family likes to go camping. We go hiking, too. We **climb** up many hills. We drink cold **water** from the stream on the trail.
We like to watch for animals in the forest. We are happy when we see **some**. You never can tell **what** kind of animals you will see.
This year we will use our **new** tent. It **could** hold an army!
I love to camp out. It's neat to see wildflowers of every **color**. I love to hear the gurgle of the stream.
When we **come** home, we think of our camping trip every **now** and then. Then we all say, "Oh boy, we **were** the best campers ever!"

Launching Instructions for the PC	Launching Instructions for the MAC
Windows Users: Insert the CD-ROM into your CD-ROM drive. The application should start in a few moments. If it doesn't follow the steps below. 1. Click on the Start button on the Desktop and select Run. 2. Type "D:\101SpellingWords.exe" (where D is the letter of your CD-ROM drive). 3. Click OK.	Macintosh Users: The CD will open to the desktop automatically when inserted into the CD drive. Double click the 101Words Flash icon to launch the program.